Every youngster needs to know how to protect himself—in school, in the playground, and in the street. Not only will the knowledge of a few self-defense techniques protect him from bullies or from real danger, but will also help build self-confidence.

Here for perhaps the first time is an instructional guide that actually shows parents how to teach their children the basics of boxing, judo, and karate purely as defensive systems. The author avoids the highly technical, the philosophical, or the mystical side of the martial arts that so often make other books on unarmed combat so difficult to read if not downright boring. A physical fitness instructor who specializes in teaching the principles of self-defense, he knows what children fear and what they are physically capable of in combatting their fears. He also includes special exercises that will help children who are especially weak to gradually increase their strength and eventually become strong.

An important feature of the book is the use of boxing as a means of self-defense. Thought of mainly as a sport, boxing is still one of the most effective combative skills and is the most easily learned. Step-by-step photographs and a brief but concise text clearly explain this and the other martial arts for the parent and child.

# TEACH YOUR CHILD SELF-DEFENSE

# TEACH YOUR CHILD SELF-DEFENSE

## DAVID MANNERS

ARCO PUBLISHING COMPANY, INC.
NEW YORK

The photographs in this book were taken by Charles Berman. The models are David Ulin, Elliott and Joel Fine, Bob and Chip Okun, and Carmine and Lora Pastore.

Published by Arco Publishing Company, Inc.
219 Park Avenue South, New York, N.Y. 10003

Library of Congress Catalog Card Number 75-13889
ISBN 0-668-03850-0

Printed in the United States of America

*To my wife Sylvia who not only encourraged me to write this book, but also helped me tremendously in preparing the manuscript.*

*To my sons Alan and Richard and my daughters Bonnie and Penny whom I admire and love dearly.*

*To my granddaughters Jessica and Rebecca whom I love very much and whose smiles light up my heart.*

# CONTENTS

# INTRODUCTION

Most boys have a fear of fighting. A parent must understand that this is a normal feeling for almost any boy. He should be made to understand that there is nothing wrong in feeling afraid. Put yourself in your boy's position. Someone comes up to you and threatens you with bodily harm. A feeling of fear will hit you immediately. Professional fighters go into the ring with a feeling of fear. So why should your son be an exception? He should be taught that nobody likes to get hurt.

I usually ask my students if they would like to get a punch in the face. They always smile and say, "Absolutely not!" Nobody likes to get hit there. The nose and the eyes are very sensitive and very easily hurt. I always assure them that their opponent does not like getting hit there either. Pain will usually discourage bullies from picking on people. When your son is taught how to fight and how to throw a hard punch directly to the eye or nose, he will usually cease to be the victim of bullies.

There are bullies in schools and in practically every neighborhood. When a bully does find someone who is afraid to fight (and mind you, he is probably afraid only because he does not know how to fight back), you can be sure that the bully will pick on this boy until the boy learns to defend himself.

Usually the type of boy who is threatened is either overweight or underweight and physically weak. A program of proper diet and exercise will help him become stronger and more physically fit. A boy who is strong and knows how to defend himself will grow up with self-confidence. This is a very important stage in the growth of the boy, so it will also help him become a more secure adult. You as a parent with the aid of this book can help your boy achieve these results. By working with your son in this manner, you will be building a closer relationship with him. He in turn will never forget what you have done for him, and when he becomes a father he will probably pass this on to his son.

# BOXING FOR SELF-DEFENSE

The first thing you must teach your child is how to clench his fist properly. Surprisingly, many children do not do this. Have him close his fingers with his thumb covering the first two fingers (see Figs. 1 and 2). Many boys make a fist with the fingers over the thumb (see Fig. 4). This is the worst way to make a fist; it is a weak one and can damage the thumb. What we want is a tight strong fist that will hurt our opponent, not ourselves. Therefore, use fist as shown in Fig. 2.

Now you will want to teach your child the boxing stance. The simplest way to teach him this is to ask him to face you with his feet 12 inches apart (see Fig. 5). Have him take a step about 12 inches forward with his left foot, keeping his knees slightly bent (see Fig. 6). Now have him hold both fists at shoulder height. The left hand extends about 12 inches from the shoulder and the right hand about 4 inches from the right shoulder (see Fig. 7). Boys who are left-handed should stand with the right foot forward and the left foot back (Fig. 8). The right hand extends 12 inches from the shoulder, the left hand 4 inches from the shoulder. This is referred to as a basic fighting position. After throwing punches at your opponent, always go back to the basic fighting position.

## FOOTWORK IN BOXING

Assume the basic fighting position. Now, you move your left foot forward first, followed by your right foot. Take short steps

11

(Figs. 9-11). This will keep you in the basic fighting position. Lefties will do the reverse. When you are retreating, you move your right foot back first, then bring your left foot back. Whenever possible try to move around on the balls of your feet. You can move much faster this way than when you are flat-footed (Fig. 12).

Another method of avoiding your opponent's punches is to circle away from him. When you are fighting a person who is right-handed, you circle to the right (Figs. 13-15). You always start to circle with the right foot first. If you start with your left foot you will cross your feet and this will throw you off balance. If he should rush you at this point, you would trip over your own feet. By circling away from a right-handed puncher, you will find that his punch will feel much lighter. If you circled toward his right hand, you would be moving toward his strength and his punches would carry more power.

You are now going to show your child how to throw a hard right-hand punch. Assume the basic fighting position (Fig. 7). The right-hand punch must be thrown with the weight of the body behind it. You accomplish this by turning your right hip toward your opponent as you throw the right-hand punch (Fig. 17). Lefties will turn the left hip as they throw a left-hand punch. When you throw a punch, whether it is a left or a right, you must hit with a snap. A punch that is thrown slowly is called a push punch. This type of punch will not hurt your opponent; instead, it will encourage him to continue to fight. When you throw your punches with speed you will hurt your opponent and this will help bring the fight to an end. It is also important to punch *through* your opponent. A punch that barely reaches your adversary has very little power (Figs. 18-19). That is why you must stay close to your opponent, if you want to hit him with power.

There are several ways for your son to practice his punching. You can hold up a pillow for him to hit (Figs. 20-22), you can hold the pillow against your body (Figs. 23-24), or you can have him hit a boxing glove (Figs. 25-26). The best method, if you own your own home and have a basement, is to purchase a heavy bag (Figs. 16-17). By practicing his punching three or four times a week, in a short time your son will be punching faster and harder. Practicing punching will build up his confidence to fight back when someone tries to pick on him.

You should buy 14-oz. or 16-oz. boxing gloves to box with your boy. Do not try to show your son what a great boxer you are. Allow your son to hit you in the body. You will hit your son back, but lightly. The boxing gloves are well padded and you probably won't feel the punches. If your son is fourteen or fifteen years of age and can throw a fairly good punch, catch the punches on the gloves (Figs. 25-26). At the beginning do not hit to the face, as nothing discourages a boy more than getting hit there. After a few weeks of body punching you can begin to hit your son with light taps to the face. This will get him accustomed to being hit. The whole point of this type of boxing is to get your son used to physical contact. After a month you can gradually hit your son slightly harder, but not hard enough to hurt him.

When your son does get into a fight, he should try to hit his opponent in the face. This way, even if your son should lose the fight, the other boy will think twice before picking on him again, since nobody likes to get hurt. The bully will probably look for someone else to pick on who will not fight back.

You must now teach your son how to block his opponent's blows. Let your son assume the basic fighting position (Fig. 7). Now throw a slow right-hand punch toward his face. He blocks the punch with his left hand. The blocking area is from the fist down to the elbow. The block is usually your wrist to his wrist (Fig. 27). After he blocks the right-hand punch with his left hand, he will throw his right-hand punch about 12 inches away from your face (Fig. 28). Now he will practice blocking with the right hand and throwing the left-hand punch (Figs. 29-30).

Next you will teach him to block with both hands. Have him place both hands (clenched fists) up to his face. Now throw slow, light punches to his blocking hands. If his blocking arms move you must tell him to hold his arms more rigid. If he doesn't, the person throwing the punches will get through to his face. After he has succeeded in this type of blocking, he must do the blocking with movement, first moving forward and backward, and then circling.

Next is body blocking. *We do not block body punches.* What we do is called counter punching. By keeping our hands high we succeed in blocking face blows but we leave our body open for body blows. When our opponent aims his punches to the body he leaves his face open to attack (Figs. 44-45). Your boy must always be on the lookout for hands that are carried low. When he sees this opening he should hit to the face immediately. Remember, nearly all fights are stopped by hitting to the face. We do have one body blow that is effective and that is a punch to the solar plexus (Figs. 48-50). This punch will render your opponent helpless and gasping for breath; his wind will be knocked out of him. This type of punch should be delivered when your opponent is only threatening you. You must strike the first blow directly to the solar plexus. You can then proceed to hit him at will because he will be helpless to stop you.

Most boys are reluctant to punch out first. They would rather wait until the other boy throws the first punch, hoping that the fight will never take place. But punching first has great advantages. First you have a clear punch to the nose, eye, or solar plexus. After the first punch you must continue punching to the face until the fight is over. It is possible that by hitting first you may not get hit back at all. (This usually happens with boys from age five to thirteen.) I usually let the boy decide for himself. You cannot make him the aggressor if he prefers to wait for the other boy to throw the first punch, but he should be advised of both procedures.

You will now teach your son how to stand before the fight starts, with his left foot slightly advanced about six inches and his hands held opened at his chest (Fig. 48). From this position he can either defend himself through blocking his opponent's blows and returning his own blows (Figs. 42-43) or he can take the initiative and strike out first. He can hit to the nose, to the eye, to the solar plexus.

He should not face his opponent with his hands at his sides or hands on his hips (Figs. 51-53), as he is leaving himself open to a punch to the face. You cannot block your opponent's punches with your hands down at your sides or on your hips.

The first punch is very important, as there is a definite advantage to the person who delivers the first blow to the face. Most fights end with one or two hard punches to the face. When you throw a strong punch to the nose, your opponent's eyes will tear and his nose will probably bleed. This will usually discourage him from continuing the fight. Remember, as soon as someone threatens you in any way bring your hands up as in Fig. 54. Be prepared either to block his punch or throw your own punch first. Your first target is his nose. Your second target is his eyes. Everybody has sensitive eyes and nose, and no one can take punishment there without feeling pain. Pain usually brings an end to a fight, and that is why I advise hitting to the nose and eyes.

Hitting to the mouth is also painful to your opponent, but it may also be painful to you. You will probably hurt his lip and make it bleed, but you will be punching his teeth, which can cause bruised knuckles.

At the beginning of a fight try to throw as many punches as you can to the face. If you see that your opponent is backing up or has been knocked off balance by your blows, follow him and keep punching. When a person is backing up or is off balance his punches will be weak. Do not give him a chance to regain his balance; keep punching at him. This will help finish the fight for you.

Remember also to keep looking for your opponent to drop his guard. This means that he has lowered his hands, leaving his face open for you to punch. During the fight you may become flustered and start to throw punches wildly. If you find yourself doing this, back off and assume the basic boxing stance as shown in Fig. 7. You will always be able to throw harder punches and block punches from the basic boxing stance. When you throw punches at your opponent, throw them straight from the shoulders (as shown in Fig. 57). Do not throw roundhouse punches (shown in Figs. 55-56). They are easier to block and are not as effective as a straight punch.

A great many fights start with your opponent giving you a shove with either one or two hands (Fig. 58). You instinctively shove him back. His response to this is to start punching you. This puts you at a disadvantage. Never shove your opponent back when he pushes you. Instead, make believe you are going to shove him back. Keep your hands open at shoulder height (Fig. 59) but as you start your hands moving toward him clench your right fist and punch him in the nose (Fig. 60). If you are a lefty, punch with your left hand.

There are times when you should avoid a fight. Do not fight if your opponent is two or three years older than you and outweighs you by thirty or forty pounds. Avoid a fight if you are bothered by a group of boys. You have to use common sense. Fight only when you think you have a chance of winning or can put up a good fight. Remember, even if you don't win, by hitting your opponent hard in the face it discourages him from picking another fight with you.

This business of fighting and being bullied usually ends upon graduation from high school. It very rarely happens when you go to work or to college.

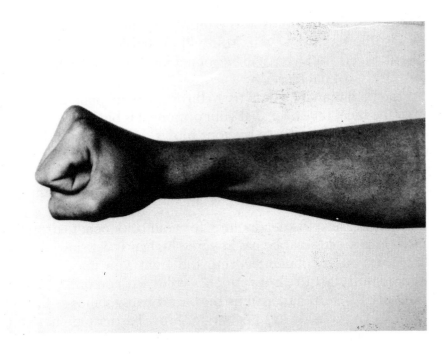

1

**Figs. 1-2**   The correct way to make a fist for boxing and karate. Practice opening and closing your fists as quickly as you can. When a fight does occur you will be better prepared to defend yourself.

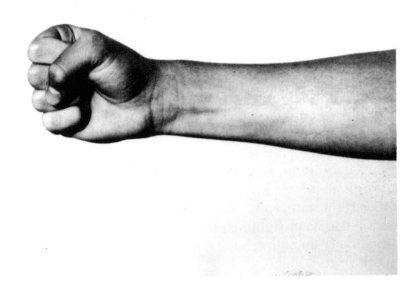

2

3

**Figs. 3-4**  Incorrect ways to make a fist. These types of fists will hurt you more than your opponent. This is why you must practice making a correct fist as in Figs. 1 and 2.

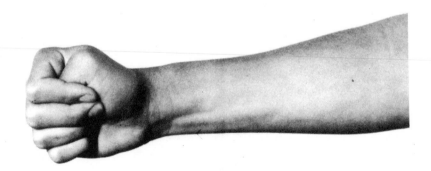

4

5

6

**Fig. 5**  Placing the child's hands in the correct position for a right-handed fighter. The right fist should be about four inches from the right shoulder and the left hand extended about 12 inches from the left shoulder. His feet should be 12 inches apart.

**Fig. 6**  The parent tells the child to step forward 12 inches with his left foot, knees slightly bent. This is called the basic fighting position.

7

**Fig. 7**  The child in the basic fighting position for a right-handed fighter.

**Fig. 8**  The basic fighting position for a left-handed fighter.

8

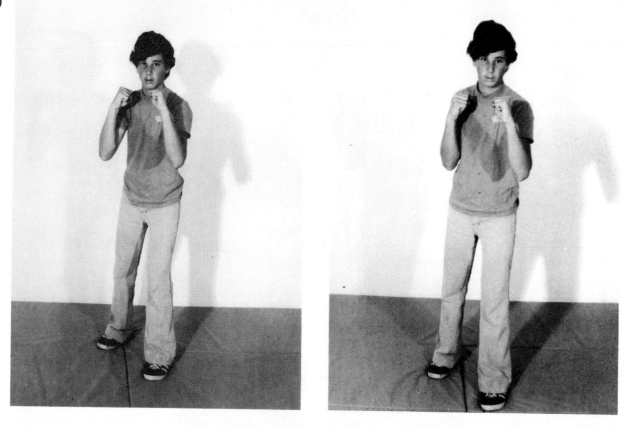

9

10

**Figs. 9-11** When advancing toward your opponent, always move forward with your left foot followed by your right foot. Take short steps. When backing up, always start back with your right foot and then your left foot, taking short steps.

11

**12**

**Fig. 12** Boxing should be done on the balls of the feet. Your heels are slightly raised off the floor as is shown in Fig. 12. You can move much faster in this manner.

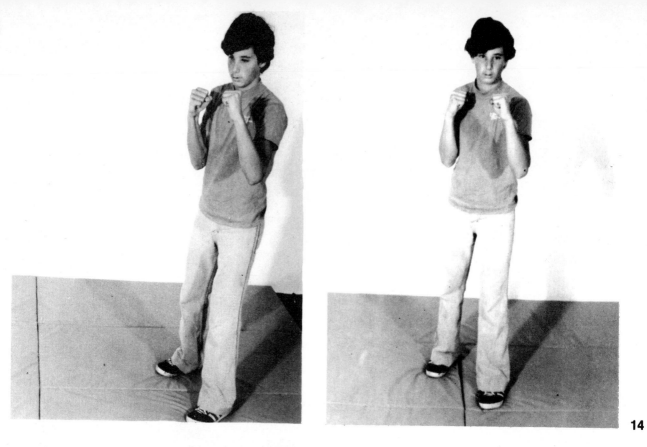

**13**  **14**

**Figs. 13-15**  When you are fighting with a person who is right handed, circle to the right, always starting with the right foot. If you start with your left foot you will trip over your own feet. Your opponent's punches will carry less power if you are circling away from his right punch. When fighting a left-handed fighter, circle to the left.

**15**

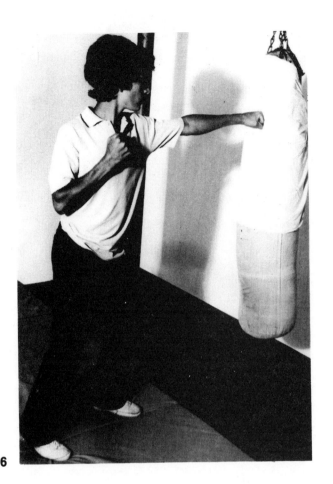

16

17

**Figs. 16-17** Right- and left-hand punching against a heavy bag. If you have a basement, a heavy bag is the best equipment you can use for boxing and karate.

**18**

**Figs. 18-19** When throwing a punch at your opponent you must be close enough so that your punch will go "through" him (Fig. 18). Should your punch just reach him, as shown in Fig. 19, you would lack power in your punch. To hit him with power, always stand close to your opponent.

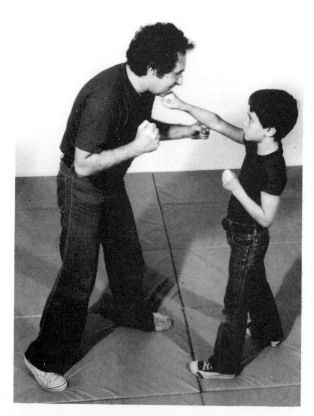

**19**

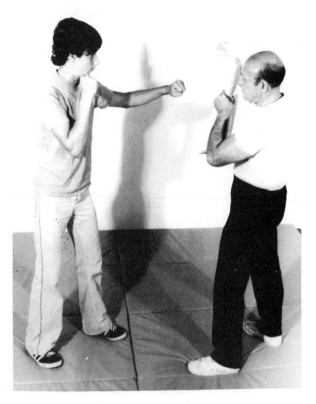

**20**

**Figs. 20-21**  Practice left-hand jab on a pillow held away from the body. The left jab is a short, fast, snappy punch. This punch is used to keep opponent away from you.

**21**

**22**

**Fig. 22** After jabbing with the left hand as shown in Figs. 20 and 21, you now throw your right-hand punch. Practice throwing left- and right-hand punches with speed and power.

**Figs. 23-24** Practice right- and left-hand punches on a pillow held against body.

**25**

**Figs. 25-26**   Practice throwing left- and right-punches against the parent's boxing gloves. Throw your right glove to his right glove and your left to his left glove. When practicing your punches, start off punching lightly and gradually increase the power of your punches. Remember, put snap into your punches. Push punches will never hurt anyone. The parent should feel that his child is throwing punches with some power.

**26**

27

**Fig. 27**   A left-hand block from a right-hand punch with boxing gloves.

**Fig. 28**   After blocking a right-hand punch, the child throws his right-hand punch to opponent's nose.

**29**

**Figs. 29-30**   The child blocks with his right hand and follows through with a left-hand punch to the nose.

**30**

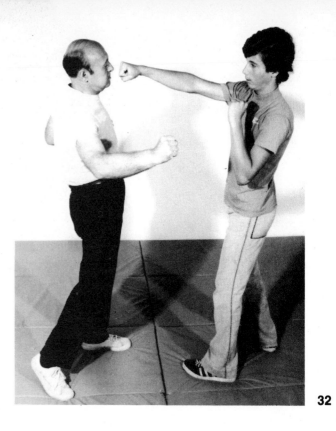

**31**

**32**

**Figs. 31-34**  These punches and blocks are the same as in Figs. 27-30, but done without boxing gloves. This is how you will be fighting in the street.

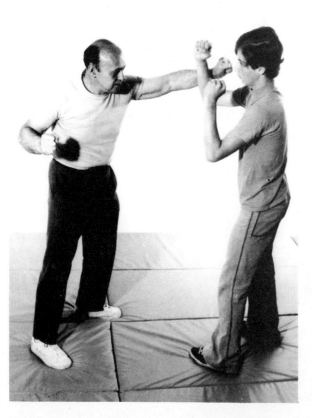

**33**

**34**

**35**

**Fig. 35** This hands-up position is an important part of your self-defense. You assume this position as soon as someone threatens you. From this position you can either block your opponent's blows or you can take the offensive as shown in Fig. 37.

**Fig. 36** The opponent is standing with his hands on his hips. The other boy is standing with his hands held at his chest.

**36**

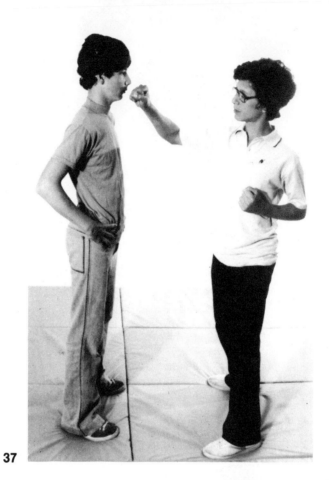

**37**

**Fig. 37** The boy on the right has now taken the offense. He is punching his opponent in the nose with his right fist. He must follow this up with a left punch. He should keep punching at his opponent until he or she has had enough. Taking the offense will surprise your opponent and will help to end the fight sooner.

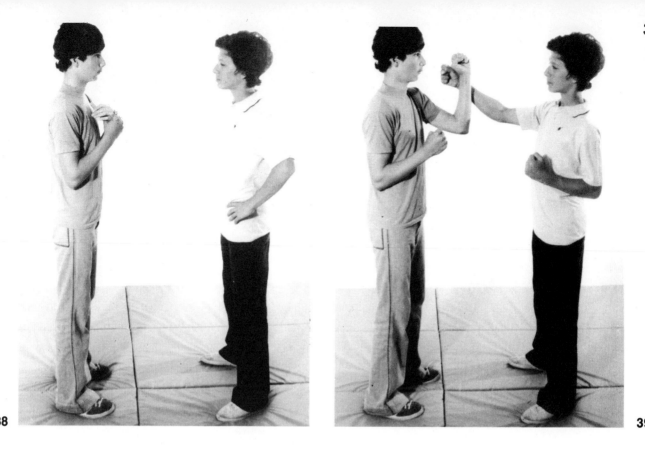

38

39

**Figs. 38-40**  The boy on the left is waiting for his opponent to throw the first punch. He throws a right-hand punch and the boy blocks with the left hand and counters with his right-hand punch to the nose. He must continue to throw punches at his opponent until the fight is over.

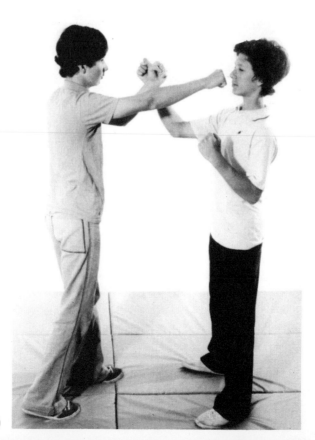

40

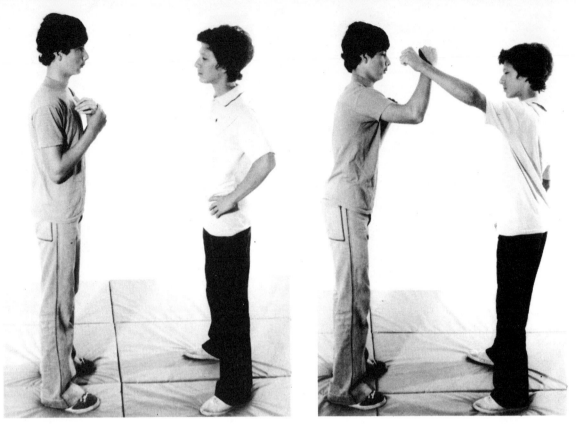

41                                                                              42

**Figs. 41-43**    These photos are the same movements as shown in Figs. 38-40, except
the boy on the left is now blocking with his right and countering with a left-
hand punch to the nose.

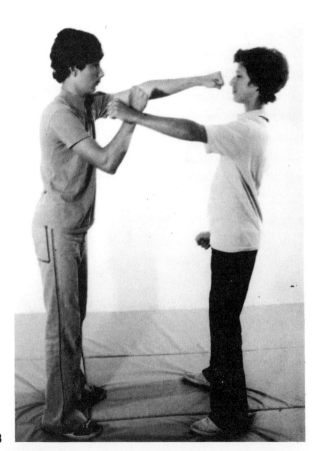

43

44

**Figs. 44-45**    Fig. 44 shows your opponent hitting to your body with his left hand. Do not try to block his punch to the body. Instead, counter with your right-hand punch to the nose or eye. In Fig. 45 your opponent is attempting a right-hand punch to the body. You counter with a left to the nose or eye.

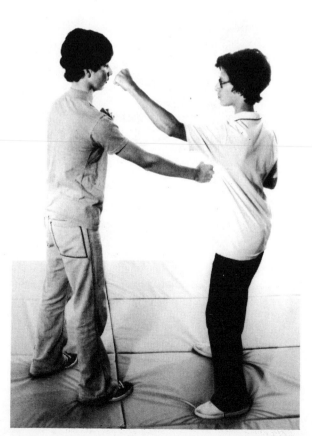

45

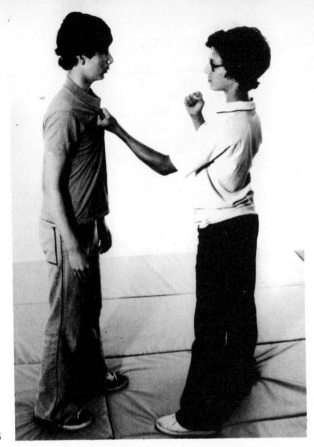

**46**

**Figs. 46-47** Your opponent has grabbed you by the shirt with his left hand (Fig. 46) and is threatening to hit you with his right fist. You counter this by punching to the nose or eye (Fig. 47).

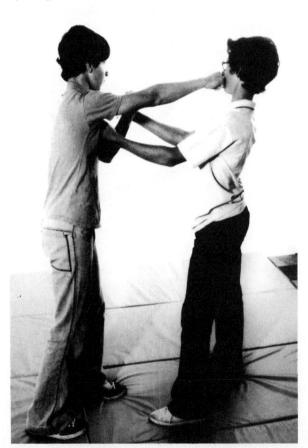

**47**

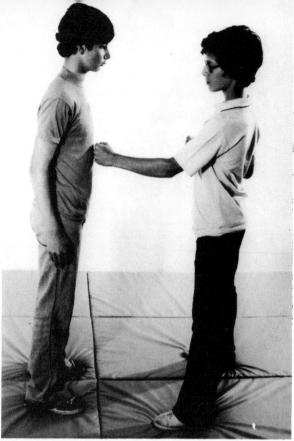

48

49

**Figs. 48-50** From the hands-up position you suddenly hit your opponent in the solar plexus with your left fist, knocking the wind out of him. You follow this up by punching to the eye or nose with your right fist. Left-handed people use right fist to solar plexus, left hand to nose.

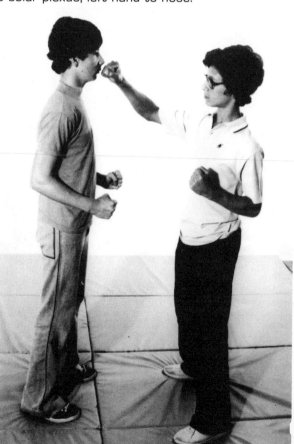

50

51

52

**Figs. 51-54** Figs. 51-53 demonstrate how not to stand when preparing for a fight. You cannot defend yourself or take the offensive from these positions. You can get hit suddenly and the fight could be over before you know what is happening. That is why I recommend the hands held up high as in Fig. 54. You are now ready to block or hit out first. Once the fight starts you assume the basic fighting position as is shown in Fig. 7.

55

56

**Figs. 55-57**  Figs. 55-56 show a right roundhouse punch. This type of punch is usually easy to block. Try to throw straight from the shoulder punches as shown in Fig. 57.

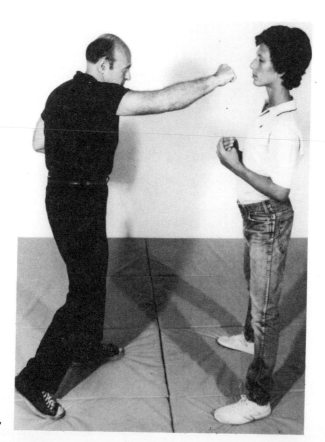

57

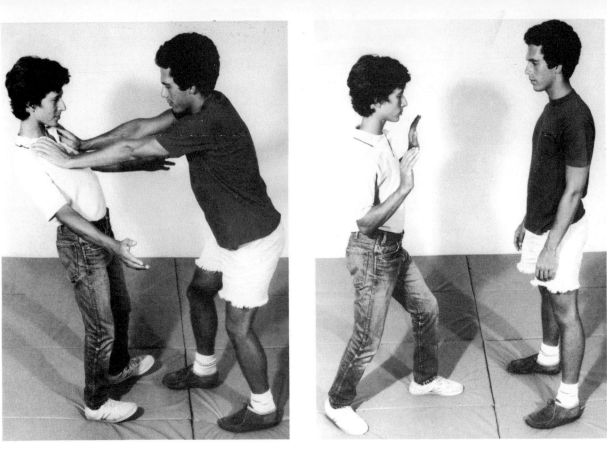

58

59

**Figs. 58-60**    Your opponent pushes you with both hands (Fig. 58). You make believe that you are going to push him back by holding both your hands open (Fig. 59), but instead you punch to the nose (Fig. 60). Remember to keep punching until the fight is over.

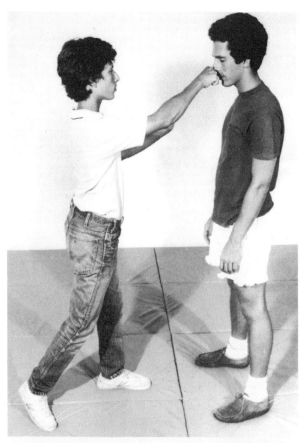

60

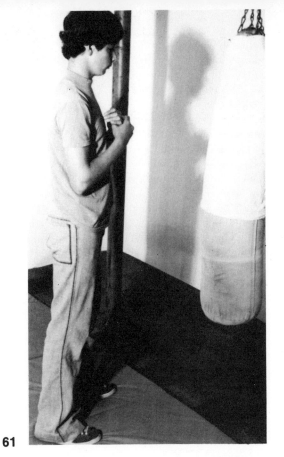 

61
62

**Figs. 61-63** Practicing on the heavy bag. Fig. 61, hands-up position. Fig. 62, left-hand punch to solar plexus. Fig. 63, right-hand punch to nose or eye. When hitting to the solar plexus do not bring your fist back before hitting your opponent. Punch straight out to your target.

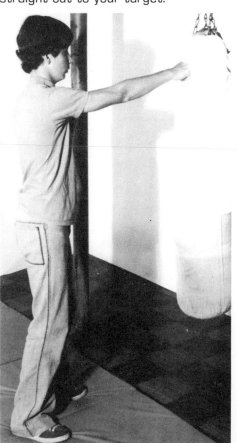

63

# KARATE

Karate is a form of self-defense that makes use of fists, fingers, feet, elbows, etc. It is a more powerful and destructive form of fighting than boxing or judo. The parent must caution his child to first try to use boxing or judo to defend himself. Karate should be used only when absolutely necessary, as when your opponent is older or larger or when there is more than one person attacking you.

A karate chop to the face has much more force than a boxing punch. A punch to the nose usually leads to a bloody nose; a hard karate blow can also break the nose. A strong front kick to the knee could dislocate the knee cap. A powerful sidehand chop to the front neck could possibly kill (when executed with medium power, it will only cause loss of breath). Karate is a self-defense weapon that must be used with caution and common sense. Children between six and twelve usually do not possess the power and weight that could produce such drastic results. However, I would still caution the child to use boxing or judo to get him out of his predicament. There are some boys who can only use karate to defend themselves. These children are usually poorly coordinated. They have difficulty in making a proper fist. They throw very weak punches. I have found that these children fight much better with open hands. If you feel that your child belongs to this group, then by all means allow him to use karate tactics.

You have shown your child how to make proper fist for boxing. Now you must demonstrate how to fight using karate

43

weapons—open hands, first two knuckles of fist, elbows, fingers, and various types of kicks.

The proper way to fight with open hands is to hold your fingers straight. They should not be bent. The side of the hand becomes hard when the fingers are held straight (Fig. 65) and becomes softer when the fingers are bent. The thumb must be kept slightly bent and next to the index finger. Karate blows are delivered with speed and with a wrist snap. When your child is practicing his karate blows on a heavy bag or pillow, you must supervise him. First see to it that his chops and punches carry some power. If you find that his hitting is weak, advise him to put more speed into the blows. It would be an excellent idea for you to work out each karate blow before showing it to your youngster. Practicing with your child will be of immense help to you, for there may come a time when you also may have to defend yourself.

Karate tactics are designed to stop most fights immediately. A prolonged fight in the end would find both participants in bad shape. The main idea in a fight is to end it quickly with one or a combination of blows. The sooner you end the fight the less chance there is of your getting hurt. Striking certain areas of the body will render a person helpless. Hitting to the center of the front neck or to the solar plexus will cause loss of breath and helplessness. When you hit a person in these areas he becomes temporarily paralyzed. Then you can hit him anywhere you want to and there is nothing he can do until he regains his ability to breathe. Another area which will cause extreme pain and helplessness when kicked is the groin. No matter how big or strong your opponent is he will not be able to withstand a kick in this part of the body. This incidentally is a good defense for girls; they should learn to be adept at kicking to this spot. This type of kick will put the opponent out for at least fifteen minutes, if not longer. However, the parent must caution the child to use this kick only as a last resort. Another time you can use a kick to the groin area is when you are being choked from the front (Figs. 128-130). Instinctively you want to pry the hands apart so you can breathe. This is the wrong thing to do, because the leverage is against you. It is much simpler to lift the hands upwards—the leverage will be in your favor—and follow through with a kick to the groin.

You can hit with much more power from the side position than from the front. Your targets would be the nose (Fig. 122), the neck (Fig. 126), or the solar plexus (Fig. 114). You can hit with the open hand (Fig. 122) or clenched fist (Fig. 116), and with either the left or right hand. You can attempt the side hit by turning your body to either the left or right. You always use the hand that is closest to your opponent. The side hit can also be used when you are either pushed or hit and you find your body facing sideways. Remember to hit with the hand nearest your opponent (Fig. 121).

Kicking is considered by most people as a cowardly way of fighting. However, kicking is an important part of karate, and we will be learning simple types of kicks, such as front kick to shin or groin, back kick to shin, or knee and downward kick to instep. Kicking, like punching, must be done with a snap. The front kick is much easier to teach than the back kick. When showing your child the front kick, be sure that he or she does not telegraph the kick by first bringing the foot back before kicking. A good example would be the kick to the groin. Assume the basic fighting position (Fig. 135). As your opponent approaches, put your weight on your back right leg and kick with your left forward foot. We use the left forward foot because it will not be seen by your opponent when you deliver the kick to the groin (Fig. 136). The closer your forward foot is to your adversary the less chance he has to block your kick. Your left forward foot will not have as much power as your right rear foot, but you do not need power in a kick to the groin.

The back kick is a little more complicated than the front kick. The back kick should be practiced with both left and right feet. The foot should be brought twelve inches off the floor (Fig. 89) and then driven straight back, straightening out the knee. The parent will find, as I have, that most children do not straighten out their knees (Fig. 85). That is where the power lies. To correct this the parent should have the child hold onto a chair for balance and then ask the child to kick back. If the leg is not fully extended you should help straighten the leg all the way out (Figs. 86-87). Then the child will understand how far back he or she must kick. You use the back kick quite often when attacked from the rear. The target is usually the shin or knee.

Another good kick to use when attacked from the rear is a heel kick to the instep. This is made by bringing the right or left foot about twelve inches straight up and then stamping down on your adversary's toes or instep (Figs. 128-129). After delivering the back kick you must turn around and be prepared to fight.

Perhaps you will deliver a left sidehand chop to the nose and follow up with a front sidehand chop to the ear. You must always be ready to hit with combination blows. You have many weapons to use, such as chops and punches with fists, elbows, and fingers and various types of kicks.

There are some children who are pests and are very annoying. They will give you a shove or a punch in the arm just for the fun or it. They can be taken care of very simply by the middle knuckle hit. Clench your fist, letting your middle knuckle protrude. Block the middle knuckle with your thumb so it cannot move (Fig. 185). Aim your blow to the side of the ribs (Fig. 186). It is a painful blow and should stop further annoyances. Another use for the middle knuckle is to hit to the side of the thigh. Hitting the thigh bones causes extreme pain. Actually the middle knuckle hit to any bony surface will cause pain. You can employ this type of blow in your arsenal of self-defense weapons.

There will be times when your child may be attacked with weapons. This book will attempt to show how to defend against sticks, knives, and guns. However, when anyone threatens you or your child with a weapon and asks for your money, give it to him. Do not try to be a hero. Whatever money you or your child may be carrying is not worth the possibility of being killed or injured. The only time you should use karate or judo against a knife or gun is when you are actually attacked. Then there is no choice, you have to defend yourself. The counter for a right-hand knife attack to your body is as follows: Grab the attacker's back of hand with your left hand and push it away from your body. Then come in with your right hand and give your opponent the hand wrist turn and kick to the groin with the right foot (Figs. 151-154). For a left-hand knife attack you push away with your right hand, then come in with your left hand and give hand wrist turn and kick to the groin. Use the same method for a gun attack.

Always use an X block (Fig. 148) plus a kick to the groin for all weapon attacks to the head. This is made in the following manner: Step forward with your left foot, body leaning towards the assailant. Then thrust both hands up, blocking your opponent's wrist, arms straight, right wrist over left wrist (Fig. 149). Now kick opponent in the groin with right foot (Fig. 150).

The only way you are going to be proficient against weapon attacks is to practice at least two or three times a week. When practicing the groin kick, do not come too close to your target.

Constant repetition will permit you to make your self-defense moves automatically.

Females have more difficulty in defending themselves. They are usually smaller and weaker than their male attackers. Karate is their best means of self-defense. It is very important that they hit or kick to certain areas of the body or face that will paralyze their assailants. Kicking to the groin (Fig. 172) will stop almost any male aggressor. It is very important that they practice this type of kick with either foot at least three times a week. Hitting a side chop to the front neck (Adam's apple), as in Fig. 179, will also render him helpless for a short period of time. The side chop is made using the outside of the open hand. There will be times when you have to use either hand for the side chop. On the left side, bring your left hand to the right shoulder and strike out to the Adam's apple. On the right side bring your right hand to the left shoulder and do the same. You must follow the side chop to the neck with a kick to the groin. This combination of side chop to neck and kick to groin will enable you to walk away from your assailant. Most women cannot outrun a man, so it is advisable to finish off your attacker.

All women should carry a police whistle in their pockets or purses. This type of whistle will frighten most assailants. Remember, when you are attacked, try not to panic. Try to recall the areas that are most vulnerable such as the groin, the eyes, the front neck (Adam's apple), and the solar plexus. Whatever counter measures you decide to use, try to finish him off with a kick to the groin. You can also try carrying salt in your purse or pocket. If you should get the opportunity, throw the salt into his eyes. Even if it doesn't succeed he will throw both hands up to protect his eyes, and you will have the opening for a kick to the groin.

Although we have a small section addressed to women in this book, there is no reason why they cannot practice all the self-defense moves. It would also be very helpful to do the exercises, which will help make you stronger, shapelier, and more physically fit.

Everyone should practice often because it will help him or her defend themselves instinctively when attacked. When you can protect yourself in this manner, it will help you tremendously in developing self-confidence.

64

**Fig. 64**   The wrong way to hit a forehand chop. The thumb should not be held away from the fingers. You could injure your thumb if you hit in this way.

**Fig. 65**   This is the correct way to hit a forehand chop. The thumb is tucked underneath the index finger. The four fingers should be held straight and not bent.

65

66          67

**Figs. 66-67**   Practicing the forehand chop on the heavy bag. This right-hand chop is
done from the right ear. Hit toward the top of the bag as though it was a
face. Strike with speed and snap. As soon as you hit the bag bring your hand
back to your ear and hit again. Try to turn your right hip and right shoulder
as you strike the bag. You should practice hitting the bag eight to ten times
a session, gradually working up to about 20 hits. Begin by hitting lightly and
increase the power of your hit as you near the end of your hitting practice.

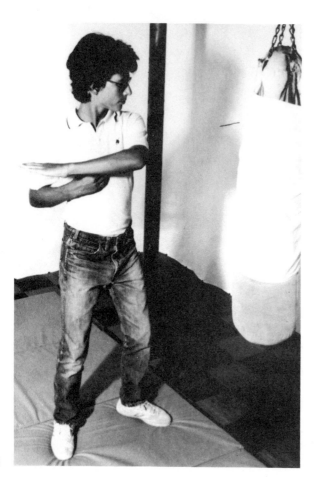 

**68**

**69**

**Figs. 68-69** Practicing the sidehand chop with the left hand on the heavy bag. This hit is made by bringing your left hand to your right shoulder and striking the bag high for a face blow. Always hit the bag with speed and snap. You can hit with more power when you put your weight on your left forward foot. Also practice the sidehand chop with the right hand.

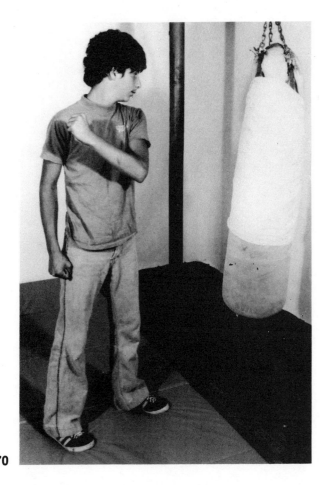 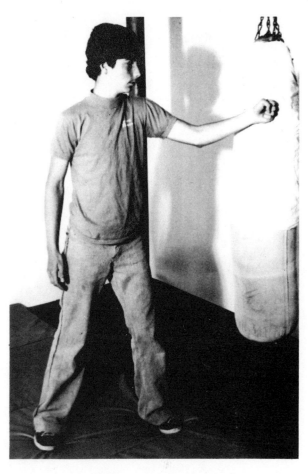

**70**
**71**

**Figs. 70-71**   Practicing the backhand hit on the heavy bag with the left fist. This blow is made from the right shoulder to the top of the bag, where your opponent's nose would be. Hit with speed, power, and with a snap, and try to come off the bag quickly. After hitting with the left, turn around to the other side and do the same with the right fist. Also practice the backhand hit to the center of the bag, the area of the opponent's solar plexus.

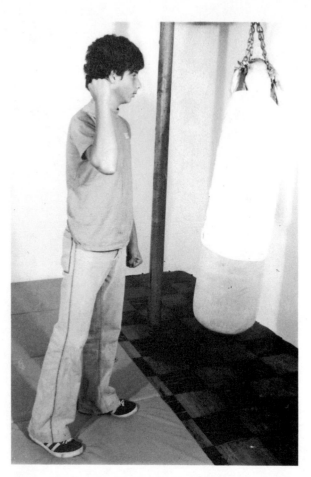

**72**

**73**

**Figs. 72-73** Practicing the hammer blow on the heavy bag. This type of hit is called the hammer blow because it is similar to hammering a nail in the wall. The hammer blow is only used for a hit to the nose. Practice hitting near the top of the bag. You hit from the right ear downward with speed and power and come off the bag quickly. Use the side of your right fist in the hammer blow. Lefties use their left hand.

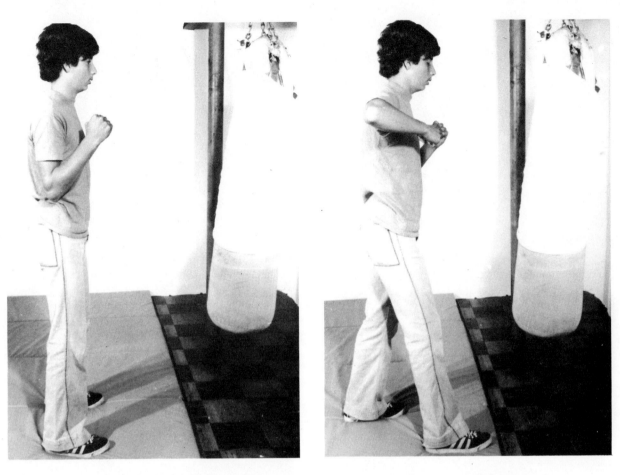

**74**

**75**

**Figs. 74-77** Practicing the right elbow hit on the heavy bag. Fig. 74 shows hands-up position, feet parallel about 12 inches apart. Fig. 75 shows right elbow has been raised to shoulder height. Fig. 76 shows elbow making contact with

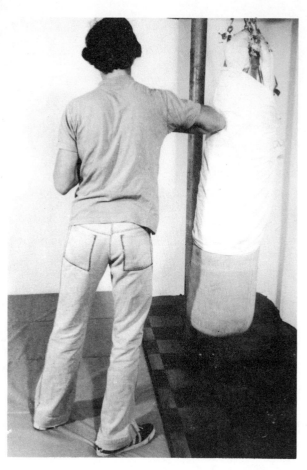

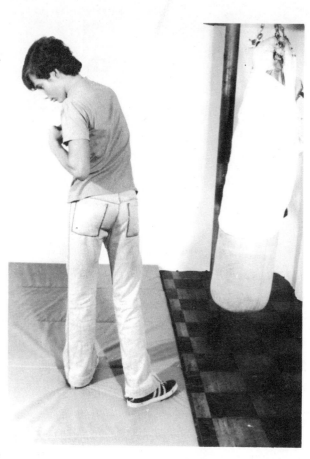

**76**

**77**

bag. In Fig. 77 elbow has gone past the bag. This hit is aimed for the left side of your opponent's jaw. The elbow hit is made with one continuous motion using speed and power. The elbow hit can also be practiced on a pillow held up by the parent.

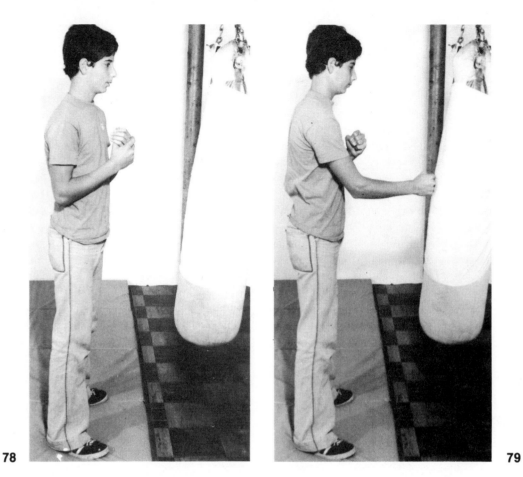

**78**

**79**

**Figs. 78-81**  Practicing the combination right-hand punch to the center of the bag and left elbow hit high on the bag. When hitting your opponent, your first blow would be right-hand punch to the solar plexus, left elbow to side of jaw. Fig. 78 shows hands up position. Fig. 79 shows right-hand punch to center of

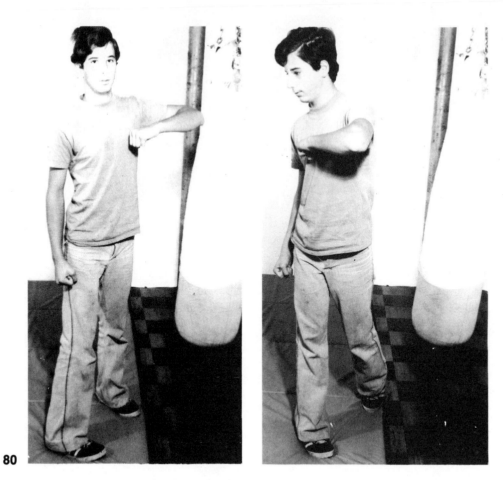

80                                                81

bag. Fig. 80 shows left elbow hit high on bag. In Fig. 81 elbow has swept past the bag. You must always follow through after making contact.

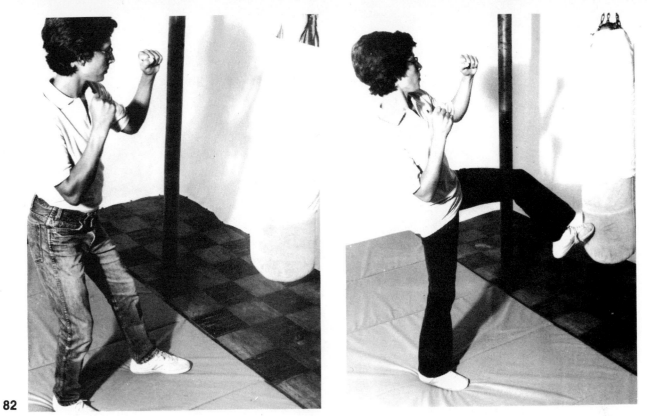

82

83

**Figs. 82-84** Practicing combination left-foot kick to groin and right-foot kick to shin or knee on heavy bag. Fig. 82 shows the basic fighting position. In Fig. 83 the weight rests on the right foot as you kick to the lower part of the bag (groin) with your left foot. Follow this with a right foot kick underneath the bag (shin), as in Fig. 84. The left-foot kick to the groin does not need much power, but the right-foot kick to the shin does.

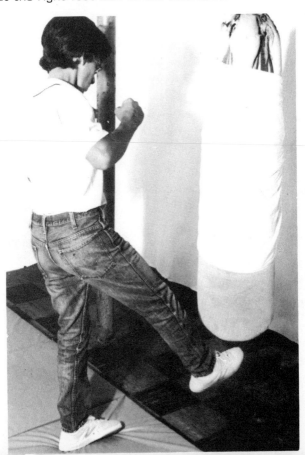

84

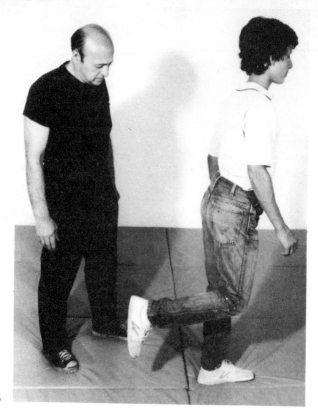

**85**

**Figs. 85-87**   The back kick is a good defense against an attack from behind. Fig. 85 shows the wrong way to kick backward. You must follow through all the way. Fig. 86 shows the parent straightening out the child's foot, showing the child how far out he must kick. Fig. 87 shows the correct back kick.

**86**                                                      **87**

**88**

**89**

**Figs. 88-90**    Practicing the right foot back kick on heavy bag. Keep your back to bag, feet parallel about 12 inches apart (Fig. 88). Bring right foot up about 12 inches off the floor (Fig. 89). Snap foot straight back, kicking with the heel of your shoe (Fig. 90). You use this type of counter when someone grabs you from behind. Practice back kick with left foot.

**90**

**91**

**92**

**Figs. 91-92** Practicing the left backhand hit on pillow. This blow is delivered from the right shoulder with the left fist. Hit the pillow with power and speed. Snap the fist off the pillow quickly. Practice with right and left hands.

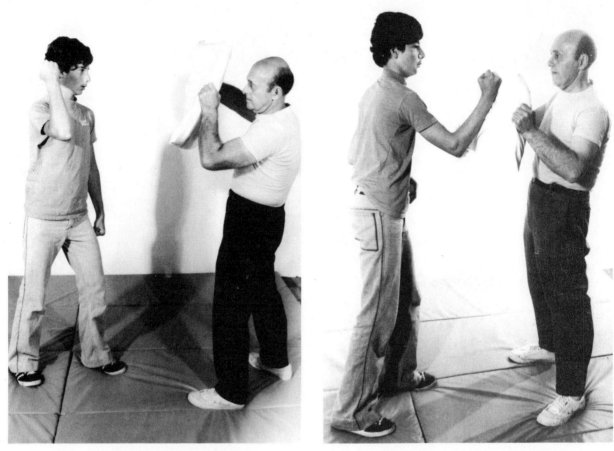

**93**

**94**

**Figs. 93-94**   Practicing the right fist hammer blow on pillow. This hit is for the nose only. You use the side of the fist and hit from the ear downward with speed and power. Snap fist back quickly.

95

96

**Figs. 95-96**   Practicing the left side hand chop on pillow. This blow should be used when you are pushed or punched into a sideways position. You can hit to the nose, chin, or solar plexus. Practice this hit with your right and left hands.

97      98

**Figs. 97-98**    Practicing the right hand chop on pillow. This blow is to the nose, eye, temple, or ear. You must try to hit with speed, power, and snap.

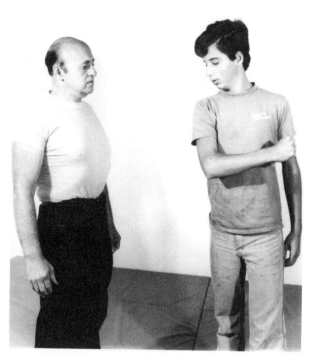 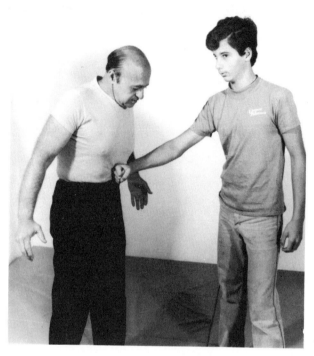

99

100

**Figs. 99-100** The right backhand hit to solar plexus. Bring your right fist back to left side under your chest, then hit your right fist to opponent's solar plexus.

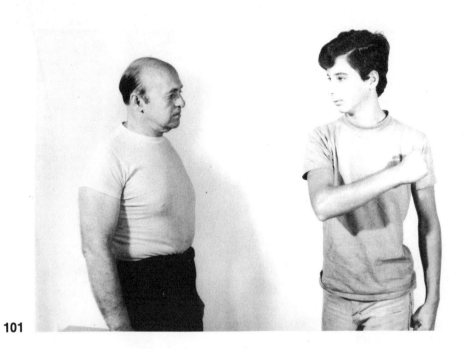

101

**Figs. 101-102**    The right backhand fist to nose. Bring your right fist back to your left shoulder, then hit it to your opponent's nose. Always hit with a snap.

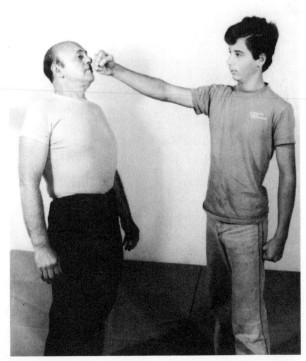

102

**103**

**104**

**Figs. 103-106** The karate right-hand punch can be practiced on the heavy bag or a pillow. Fig. 103 shows the first position for practice of the karate punch. This hit is made with the first two knuckles of the hand. Your left hand is extended straight out from the shoulder. Your right hand is held next to your ribs. Both fists are clenched. Fig. 104 shows the finish of the punch. Figs. 105-106 show same karate punch from side position. Karate hitting power is achieved by both right and left fists moving at the same time. If you punch first with the right hand and then bring your left hand back, you will not have the same power as when both hands move simultaneously. Practice this karate punch in front of a mirror. Make sure both hands are in the correct finishing position, right fist knuckles up, left fist knuckles under, as in Fig. 103. Also practice with your left hand. Practice ten hits starting with your right fist and ten starting with your left fist.

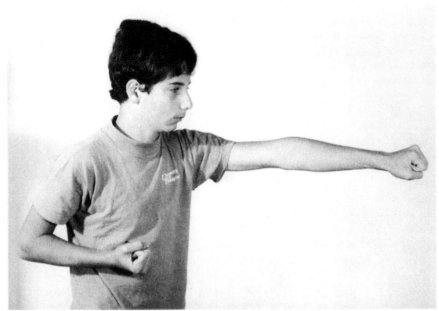

**105**

**106**

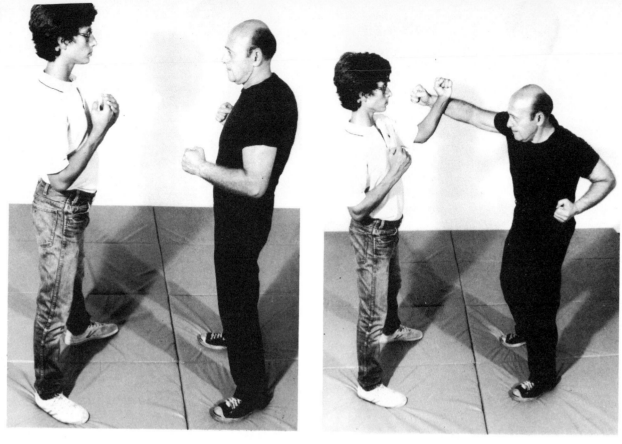

107

108

**Figs. 107-109**    Counter to a right-hand punch. Fig. 107 shows the hands-up position getting ready to block a right-hand punch. Fig. 108 shows blocking of the right-hand punch with the left hand. Fig. 109 shows the right-hand karate punch to the nose or eye. Practice blocking with the right hand and throw a left-hand karate blow to the nose or eye.

109

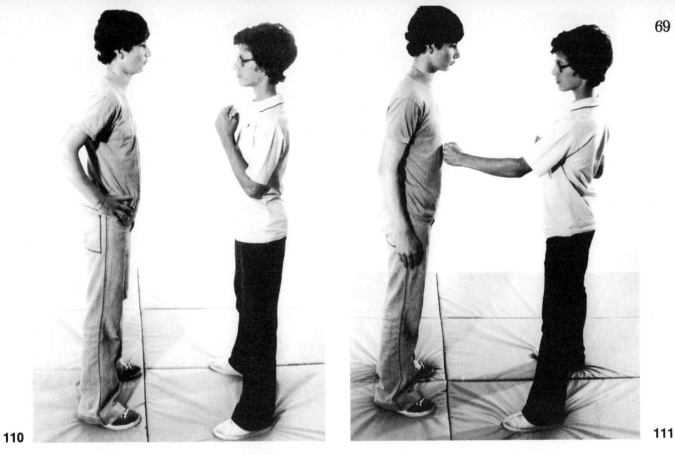

110                                                                    111

**Figs. 110-112**   Offensive combination blows. Fig. 110, hands up to chest position. Fig. 111, you suddenly hit your opponent in the solar plexus with your left fist. Follow this up with a hammer blow to the nose (Fig. 112).

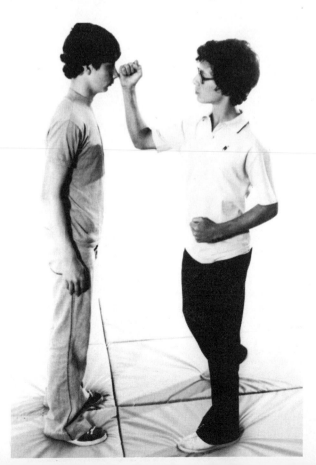

112

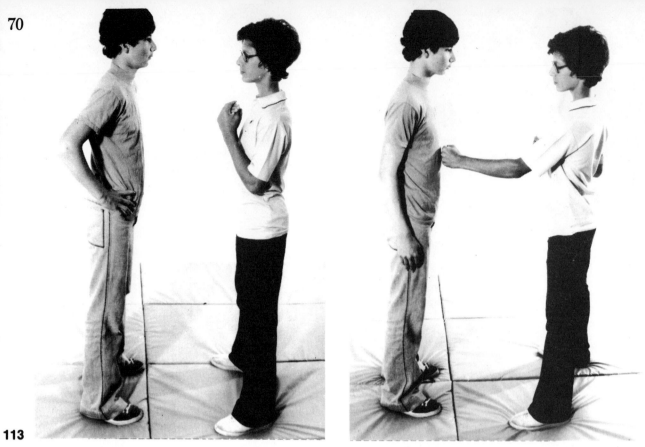

113

114

**Figs. 113-115** Offensive combination blows. Fig. 113, hands up position. You take your opponent by surprise and hit him in the solar plexus with your left fist (Fig. 114) and a right-hand chop to the nose or eye (Fig. 115).

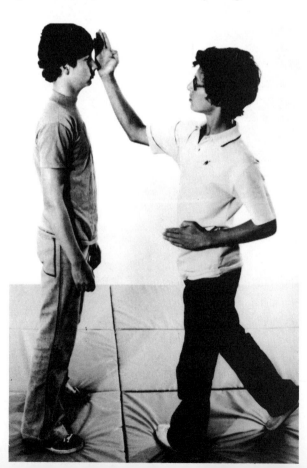

115

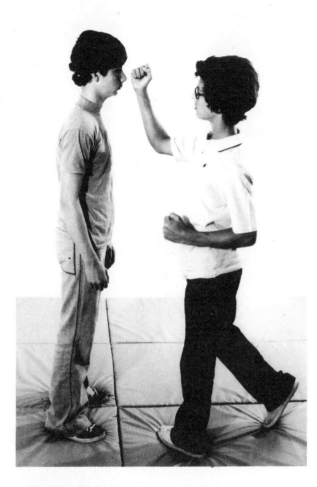

116

117

**Figs. 116-117** Offensive combination blows. This blow is used whenever you find yourself facing your opponent sideways. You hit to the solar plexus with your left backhand fist, following this up with a hammer blow to the nose.

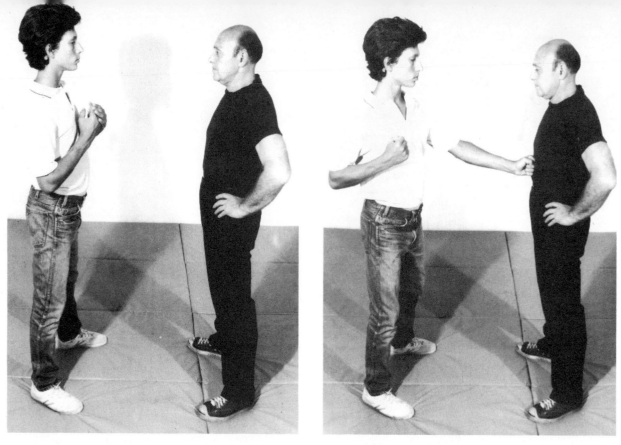

**118**  **119**

**Figs. 118-120**  Offensive combination blows. Fig. 118, hands-up position. You hit to the solar plexus with your left fist, then step in with your right foot and swing your right elbow and hit your opponent's left side of jaw. You do not stop at the jaw; you must follow through past the jaw.

**120**

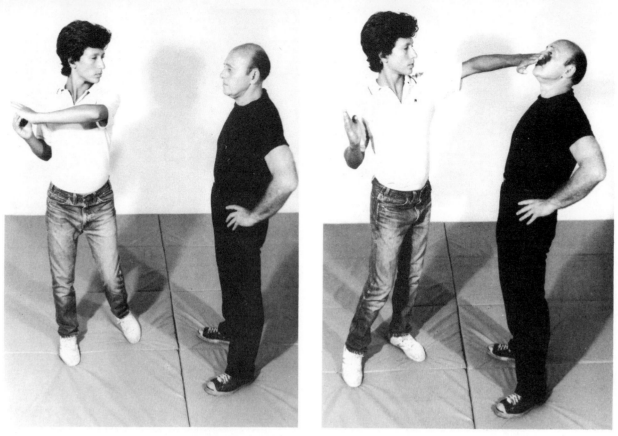

121                                                                                          122

**Figs. 121-123** The sidehand chop combination blow. Stand with your body sideways to your opponent. From your right shoulder, you hit with a left sidehand chop to the nose. Follow this with a front right-hand chop to the eye. A left-handed person would first hit with a right-hand chop to the nose followed by a front left chop to the eye.

123

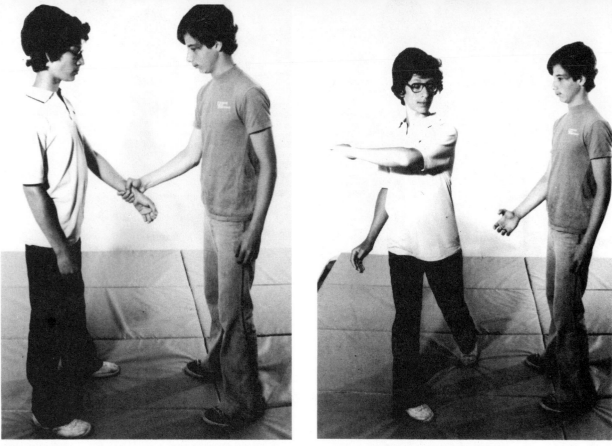

124
125

**Figs. 124-126** Counter to a wrist grab. Your opponent has grabbed your left wrist. You counter this by pulling your hands away swiftly and hitting to the Adam's apple (neck). You can also hit to the nose or solar plexus. When pulling your hand free of your opponent's grasp, always pull out and away from his fingertips.

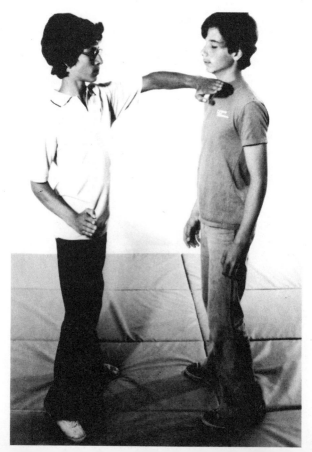

126

127

128

**Figs. 127-130** Counter to a stranglehold from behind. Your opponent has grabbed you from behind in a stranglehold. You can use one of two counters. Lift your left foot up and stamp down on your opponent's instep (Figs. 128-129) or kick back hard to his shin (Fig. 130).

129

130

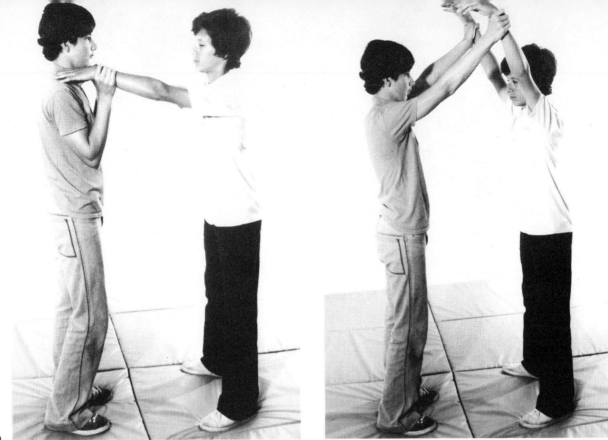

**128A**

**129.**

**Figs. 128A-130A**  Counter to a front choke (I). Your opponent has you in a front choke at arm's length. Counter this by grasping the wrists and lifting the opponent's arms overhead and then kicking right foot to groin. A person who is choking you at arm's length is in a weak position to use leverage. That is why you will find it easy to lift your opponent's hands from your neck.

**130A**

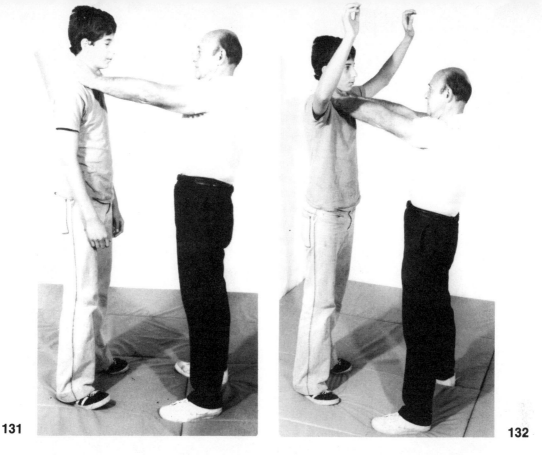

131    132

**Figs. 131-134**    Counter to a front choke (II). Your opponent has you in a front choke at arm's length. Lift both of your arms overhead and turn left quickly, breaking the choke with your right arm. From this position hit to the Adam's apple (neck) with a right sidehand chop.

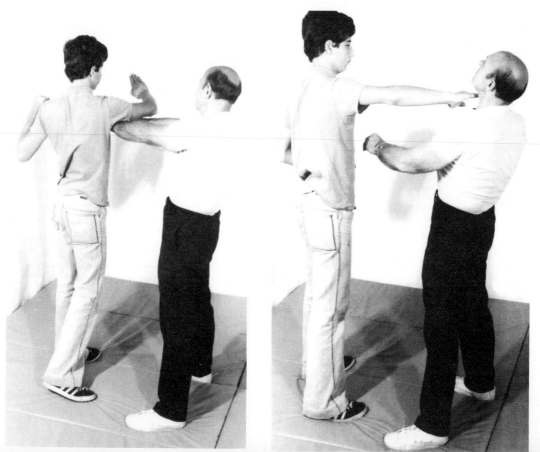

133    134

135

136

**Figs. 135-136**   Kicking to the groin from basic boxing position. Use this counter only if you are fighting an opponent who is older and bigger than you. Stand in a basic boxing stance, then put your weight on your right foot and kick to the groin with your left foot.

**137**

**Figs. 137-139** Counters to a kick to the groin. Cross your wrists (this is called an X block) and block the opponent's ankle (Figs. 137-138). Or bring your right knee up against your left thigh, crossing slightly to cover your groin (Fig. 139). This is the quickest way to block a groin kick.

**138**

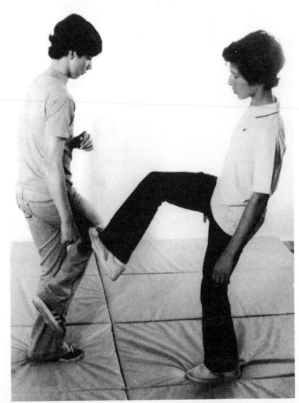

**139**

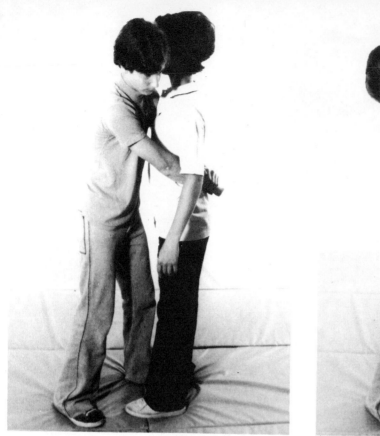

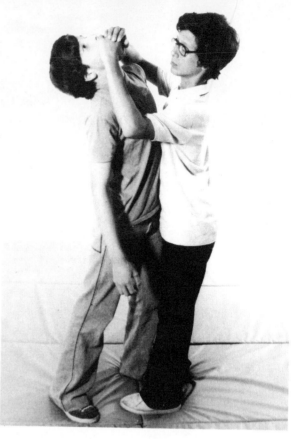

**140**

**141**

**Figs. 140-142**  Counter to a front bear hug. Fig. 140 shows a front bear hug. To counter this bring both hands up together, right hand over left hand, and place them underneath your opponent's nose and push back. This will break his hold, allowing you to follow through with a front right-hand chop to the nose.

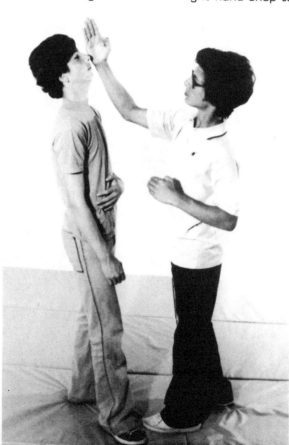

**142**

143

144

**Figs. 143-146** Other counters to a front bear hug. To counter the bear hug, you can also hit attacker's both ears with your open hands (Fig. 144). Another counter is to hit both middle knuckles to either temple (Fig. 145). Fig. 146 shows how to make the middle knuckle for hit to temple.

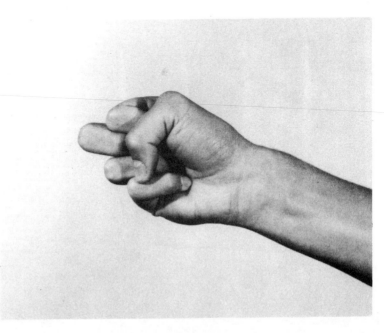

146

145

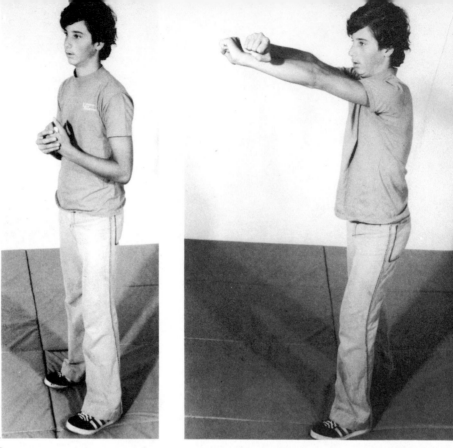

147

148

**Figs. 147-150** Counter to an overhead weapon attack. Fig. 147 shows position before attempting the overhead X block. Fig. 148 demonstrates the correct position for the overhead X block, right wrist over left wrist. Fig. 149 shows overhead X block used against a weapon; elbows should be straight and not bent. Kick to groin after using X block (Fig. 150).

149

150

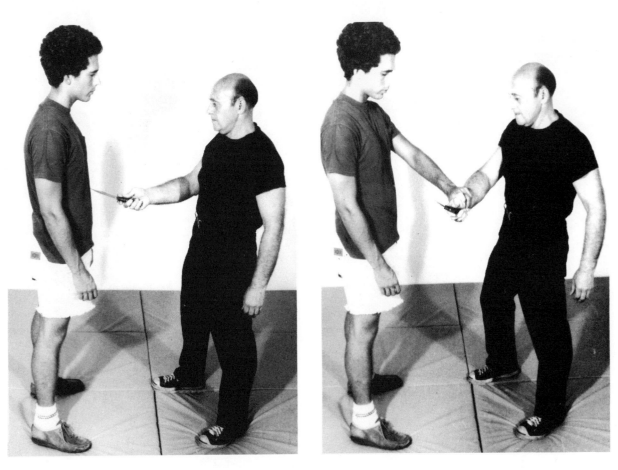

151

152

**Figs. 151-154** Counter to a knife attack. You are being threatened with a knife held near your stomach. Move your left hand slowly, close to your body, toward the knife hand. Try to move with extreme care so that the attacker does not realize that your left hand is moving towards his hand. Now quickly grab his back hand with your left hand, using an overhand grip, and push it away from

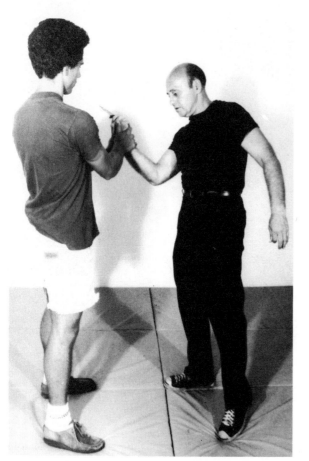

**153**

**154**

your body (Fig. 152). Come in quickly with your right hand and complete the hand wrist turn until your attacker is off balance and then kick to the groin.

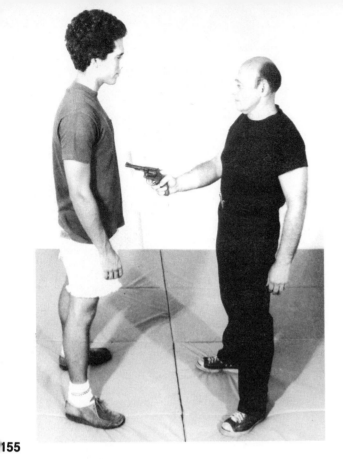

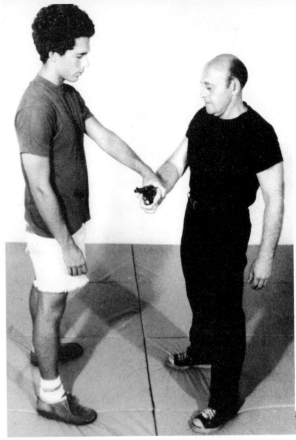

155

156

**Figs. 155-158**  Counter to a gun attack. This is made exactly the same as the counter to a knife attack.

157

158

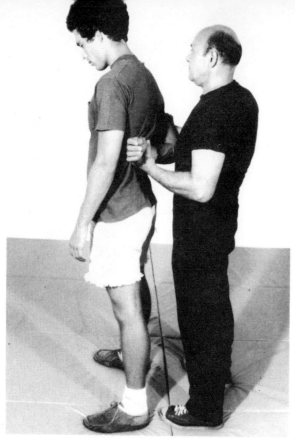

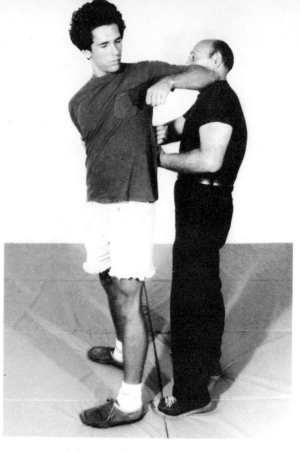

159

160

**Figs. 159-162**  Hammerlock counters. Fig. 159 shows the right-hand hammerlock position. One counter is to turn to your left side and swing your left elbow to your opponent's jaw (Fig. 160). A simple counter is to bring your left foot up and stamp down on your opponent's instep (Figs. 161-162).

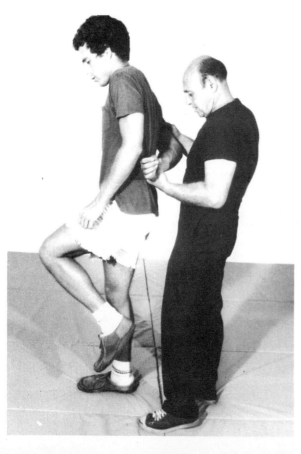

161

162

**163**

**164**

**Figs. 163-164** Headlock counter. Fig. 163 shows the headlock position. With your middle knuckle hit the center of your opponent's thigh bone on the outside of the thigh (Fig. 164). This hit is very painful when done properly. Try it lightly on yourself and you will have a better understanding of this counter.

165

**Figs. 165-167**  Counter from sitting position (I). When you are down on the ground in a sitting position, always try to face your opponent with both your feet toward him. As your opponent steps forward with his left foot, hook your left foot behind his left ankle, bring your right foot back and kick into your opponent's right knee.

166

167

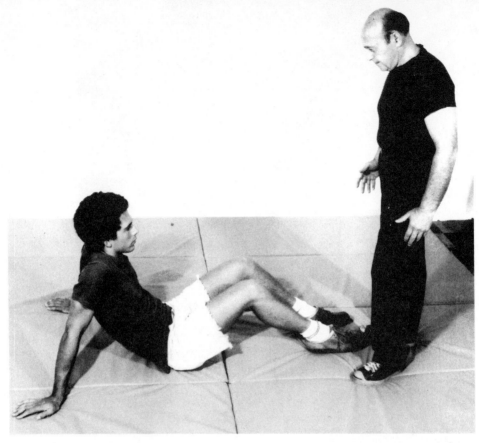

**168**

**Figs. 168-169**  Counter from sitting position (II). As your opponent steps forward with his left foot, kick to the groin with your right foot.

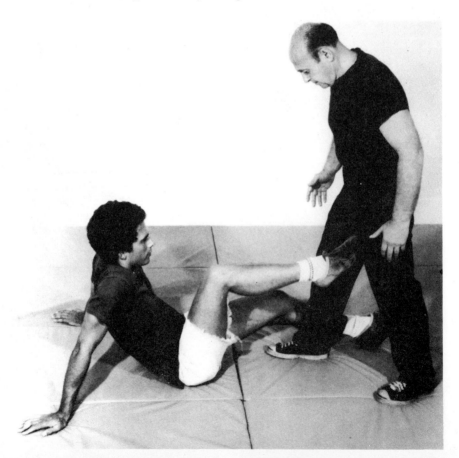

**169**

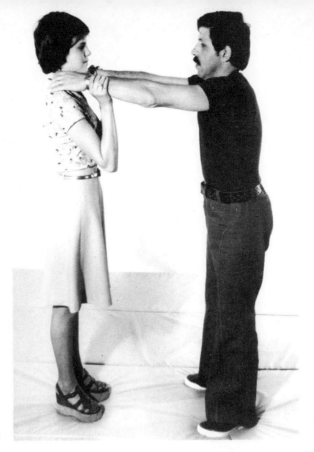

**170**

**Figs. 170-172**  Counter to a choke hold (I). When caught in a choke hold, most people try to pry the hands apart (Fig. 170). This is wrong as the leverage is against you. Figs. 171-172 demonstrate the proper way to break a choke hold. Grab the wrists and lift overhead, kicking right foot to groin.

**171**

**172**

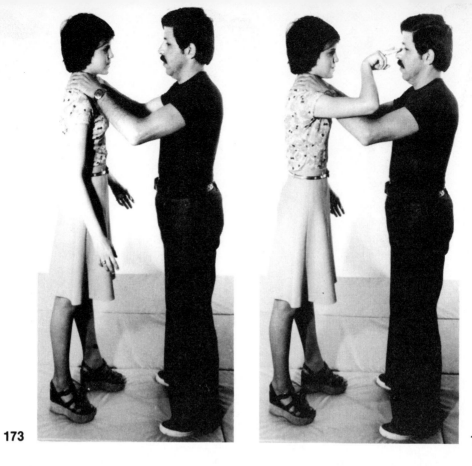

173    174

**Figs. 173-175**    Counter to a choke hold (II). Attacker is choking girl with both hands. Girl pokes two fingers into his eyes and follows with a kick to the groin.

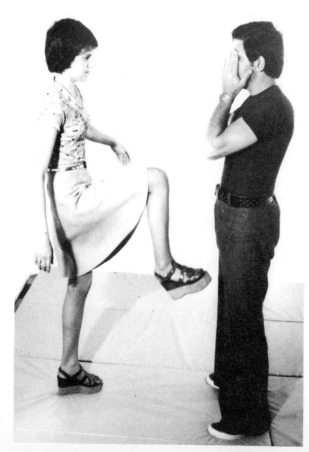

175

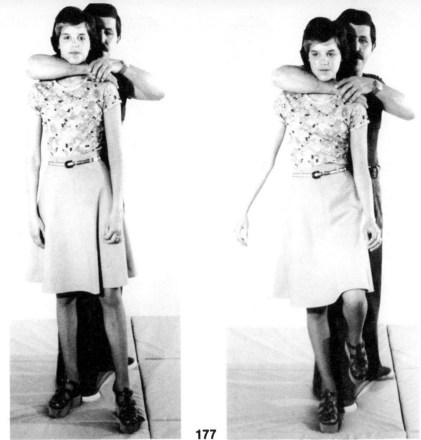

**Figs. 176-180** Counter for stranglehold from behind. Girl is being attacked from behind in a stranglehold. She counters this by lifting up her left foot (Fig. 177) and stamping down hard on the attacker's instep (Fig. 178). After being released, she hits the attacker in the throat with a sidehand chop (Fig. 179) and follows with a kick to the groin.

181

182

**Figs. 181-184** Counter to a wrist grab. If you are grabbed by the wrist by a molester, turn your body to the side and pull your wrist quickly away from his fingertips (Fig. 182). From this side position, hit to the throat with a sidehand chop and follow up with a kick to the groin.

183

184

185

**Figs. 185-186**    How to hold your fist for a middle knuckle hit. Middle knuckle hit to the side of ribs, which is extremely painful.

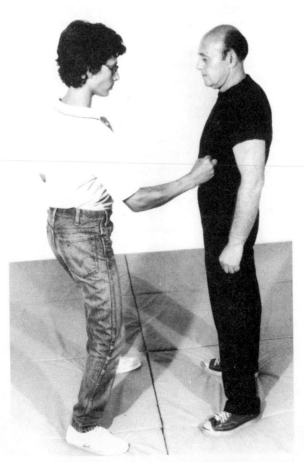

186

187

188

**Figs. 187-190** Counter to a high shoulder grab from behind. Throw your hands overhead and then hit backward with your left elbow to your attacker's solar plexus (Figs. 188-189). Follow this up by turning to the right and swinging your right elbow to his jaw (Fig. 190).

189

190

# JUDO

The parent is going to find that judo will be more difficult to teach his child than boxing or karate. It is easier to teach punching, karate blows, and kicks. Even if they are not done properly, they can still hurt your opponent, whereas a judo hold or throw not properly done will leave you in a vulnerable position. Most of the self-defense shown in this book is taken from actual situations that boys may encounter in school and in the street.

You will find that your child will be more proficient at learning certain holds or throws, and have trouble with others. If you are patient, sooner or later your child will pick up the more difficult ones. Most people who learn the art of self-defense will choose favorite holds, blows, or throws and become very proficient in their execution. It is more important to be able to do a few things well than to try to absorb an over-abundance of holds and throws.

This book deals with three types of self-defense: boxing, judo, and karate. Boxing and karate deal with punching with fists, hitting with elbows, chopping with sides of hands, kicking with feet, etc. Judo, as shown in this book, will deal only with simple holds and throws.

There will be times when you will prefer to use judo holds and throws in defending yourself. It all depends on the situation. You may find that your friends will be testing you, and it is not uncommon for friends to push, hit, and wrestle with you. When you are between ages five and eighteen friends and foes alike will be testing your strength and your ability to fight back. It is

97

not likely that you would want to punch your friends in the face, so you can use the various holds and throws shown here. If you find that the judo holds and throws are not effective, then you will have to resort to punching to the face. The use of judo will be sufficient to deter some boys, but others will require a more painful experience, such as a punch to the eye or nose, before they will leave you alone. Many of my students who have taken courses in judo have found that they could not cope with boys who threw punches at them. That is why it is best to know all three forms of self-defense: boxing, judo, and karate.

Judo is the art of using movement, balance, and leverage to throw your opponent. You also use various locks and holds to force your opponent into submission. A person can utilize his full strength when he is in a balanced position. A balanced position would be the basic boxing stance (Fig. 5) with feet spread twelve inches apart. By pulling or pushing your opponent off balance (Fig. 232) you immediately take away most of his strength. This is the time when you can throw him to the ground and it is really the only way you should attempt to throw your opponent. When you try to throw your opponent when he is in a balanced position, it is going to be a question of which one of you is stronger. By pulling him off balance there is no question that he will be the one who will be thrown.

You will find that throwing your opponent to the ground does not always end a fight. It may be necessary to follow up a throw with a punch either to the face or the solar plexus (Fig. 49). Although you can pull a person off balance when he is stationary, it is much easier to pull him off balance when he is moving towards you. An example of this would be when you are both holding each other by the shoulders. You take a step backward; he in turn takes a step forward. That is the time for you to pull him forward with your right hand and block his ankle with your left foot and throw him to the ground. It is very important to pull with strength. The more you pull a person off balance the easier it is to throw him.

The parent must teach his child the importance of balance and of being off balance. He must first pull the child off balance so that he is standing on one foot. Then pull him off balance on the other side. By doing this, you will make him realize how weak he feels from his off-balance position. Let him do the same to you (Figs. 223-224). If you have two children, have them work together while you supervise the proceedings.

One of my favorite judo holds is the hand wrist turn (Figs. 191-195). It has helped my students avoid a great many fist fights. Since most fights start with a push, this would be the perfect time to use the hand wrist turn. When it is properly executed your opponent will find himself flat on his back. You should concentrate on this particular hold, as it will be used often by your child.

## THE HAND WRIST TURN

The hand wrist turn should be made in the following manner. The parent holds his right hand up, back of hand facing child (Fig. 191). The child grasps the parent's hand with both of his hands. His thumbs are alongside each other underneath the knuckles of the hand and the fingers of both hands are holding the inside of the palm (Fig. 192). Now the child turns the hand inward in a circular fashion, concentrating on immediately pressing the last two knuckles inward. This is the most important part of the hand wrist turn. The hand should be turned at shoulder height halfway between your child and you (Fig. 193). When this hold is done properly, an opponent will feel pain in the wrist and will be forced to the ground (Fig. 194). When practicing this hold always apply pressure to the wrist gradually, otherwise the person the pressure is applied to will end up with a strained wrist.

## HEADLOCK COUNTERS

One of the favorite holds of most bullies is the headlock. This is a painful hold and a counter to the headlock is imperative. There are two counters that we will be working with. The first counter is to a side to side headlock (Fig. 214). Put your left hand around your opponent's waist as your right hand pulls back on his hands to ease the grip. Then take a short step in front of your opponent with your right foot (Fig. 215) and a long step with your left foot bringing your body in front of him. Be sure that your feet cover both his ankles (Fig. 216). Then using your left hand, which is around your opponent's waist, throw him over your left foot (Fig. 217).

The second counter is to a front to back headlock. Your

opponent has you in a headlock. You are directly behind him. Place both of your open hands on the back of his thighs (Fig. 218). Now you must sit down and then lie back in one motion. As your opponent nears your face throw him over your head (Fig. 220). When done properly this counter never fails.

Now, this is the way you use a headlock on an opponent. Place your left or right hand around his head (not the chin) (Fig. 212). Bring his head close to your ribs and squeeze hard (Fig. 213).

## RUSH ATTACK

Another common attack is called a "rush attack." Your opponent is rushing at you with outstretched hands (Fig. 252). The counter is similar to the movement of a bull fighter avoiding the bull with his cape. You step aside with either your left or right foot. Grasp your opponent with both of your hands underneath his arms near his shoulders (Fig. 253). Then throw him as far as you can (Fig. 255). The counter to the rush attack will only succeed if you grasp your adversary and step aside right before he or she is about to grasp you. The idea is to use your opponent's momentum to complete the throw.

## FULL NELSON

There is another form of attack called the "full nelson." Your attacker will come up behind you and bring both his hands under your armpits and then around your neck (Fig. 241). The counter to this is very simple. As you feel your opponent's hands coming under your arms, squeeze your elbows to your sides (Fig. 242). (Do not allow the hands to reach the neck.) Your opponent's arms will be pinned and he will be unable to execute the "full nelson."

## COUNTER FROM THE GROUND

There will be times when you will find yourself thrown to the ground. Do not under any circumstance allow yourself to fall to the ground face down. It is almost impossible to defend yourself from this position. Try to turn around and face your opponent

(Fig. 256). From this position you can use your legs or your hands to defend yourself. Always keep your feet facing your opponent. This way as he approaches you can either kick or trip him.

## THE HAMMERLOCK

The hammerlock (Fig. 209) is another favorite hold used by bullies. The counter to this hold is to bend the body forward and straighten out your arm quickly and pull it away (Fig. 211).

## WRIST GRAB COUNTER

When someone grabs your wrist (Fig. 243) you should always pull out from your opponent's finger tips (Fig. 244). Another counter is to keep your fingers together and spread your thumb apart (Fig. 245) and quickly come up under his wrist. This will break his hold and you will end up grasping his wrist (Fig. 246).

## STRANGLEHOLD AND BRING DOWN

There are times when you may want to take offensive action. This next movement is simple to execute. It is a push and pull into a stranglehold and bring down. You face your opponent with your hands up near your chest (Fig. 247). From this position in one fast motion you bring your left hand behind your opponent's right shoulder and place your right hand on his left shoulder (Fig. 248). Now pull and push with all your strength until your adversary is turned quickly around (Fig. 249). Your right arm will be held tightly against his neck. Quickly slip your left hand down to your assailant's back (Fig. 250). Push the back forward with the left hand, pull back with right hand, and bring the person down to the floor (Fig. 251).

## BRING DOWN FROM BEHIND

This is another offensive move. You come up behind your opponent and grasp both his shoulders with your hands. At the same time, place the toes of your right foot on the back of your assailant's knee (Fig. 238). Now push the back of your opponent's right knee forward and at the same time pull his shoulders back towards you sharply. As he falls, quickly jump out of the way (Fig. 240).

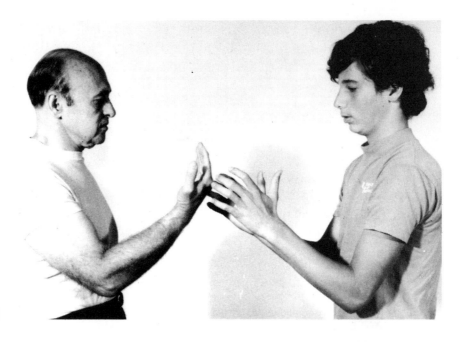

191

192

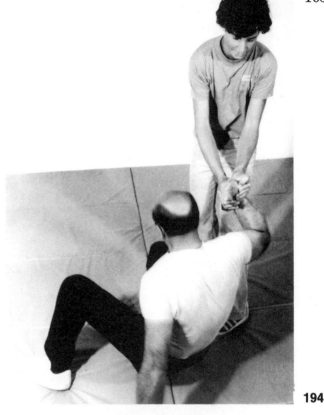

**193**

**194**

**Figs. 191-195** Hand wrist turn. Parent holds up his right hand, knuckles facing child (Fig. 191). Child grasps hand, fingers around center of hand, thumbs just below the knuckles (Fig. 192). The child twists the hand in a circular fashion inward (Fig. 193). It is important to twist and apply downward pressure to the last two knuckles. This brings pain and pressure to the wrist. The opponent is brought down to the ground by this pressure (Fig. 194). Fig. 195 shows how to apply thumb pressure on the hand. Don't forget to twist the last two knuckles inward and apply downward pressure.

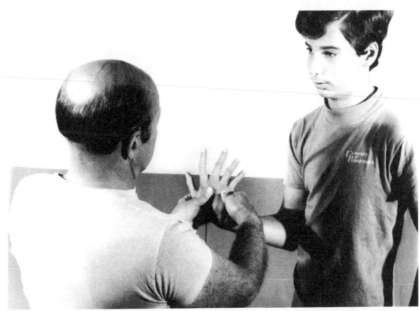

**195**

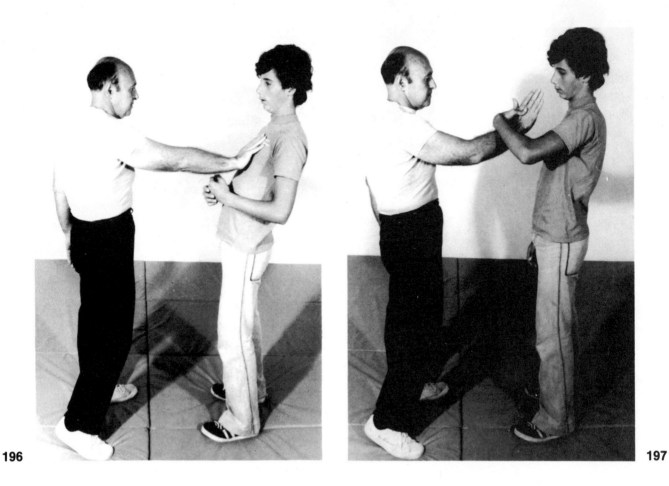

196

197

**Figs. 196-200**   Counter to a right-hand push. This is a hand wrist turn done from a right-hand push. Opponent pushes child with right hand (Fig. 196). Child grabs opponent's right hand with his left hand, thumb underneath knuckle of index finger (Fig. 197). He turns hand with his left hand so that the back of opponent's hand is facing him (Fig. 198). Now he comes in quickly with his

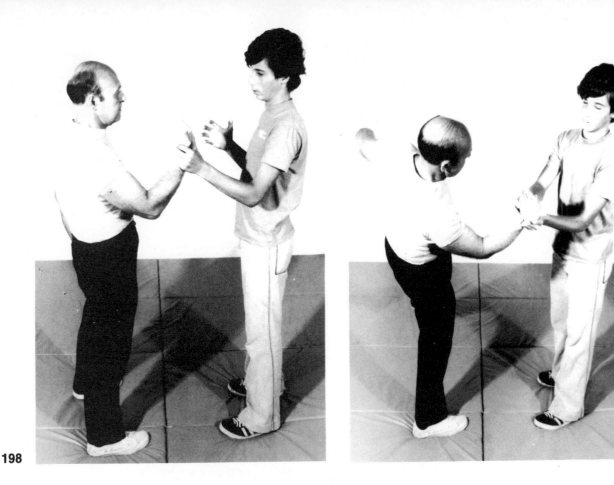

198

199

right hand, placing it alongside his left hand (Fig. 199). He twists the last two knuckles and applies downward pressure (Fig. 200). After he has his opponent down on the ground, he punches to the nose if the occasion warrants it.

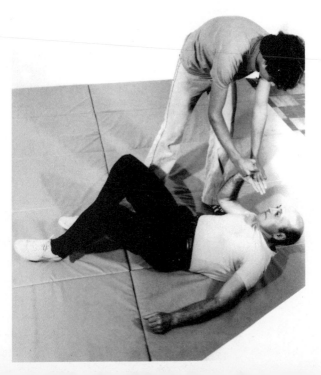

200

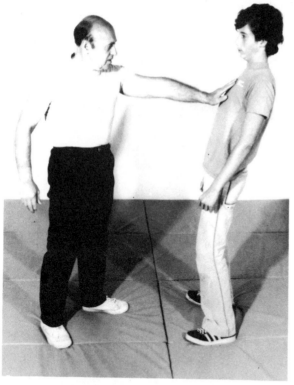

**201**

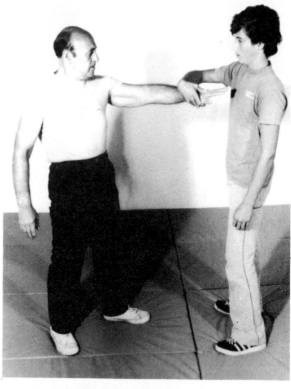

**202**

**Figs. 201-204**    Counter to a left-hand push. This is a hand wrist turn done from a left-hand push. Opponent pushes the child with left hand. Child grasps opponent's left hand with his right hand, thumb over index finger below knuckle (Fig. 202). Child comes in quickly with his left hand, placing it alongside the right hand, twisting inward and applying pressure downward (Fig. 203), twisting down to the floor and punching to nose if necessary. Incidentally, on a two-hand push always attack the right hand.

**203**

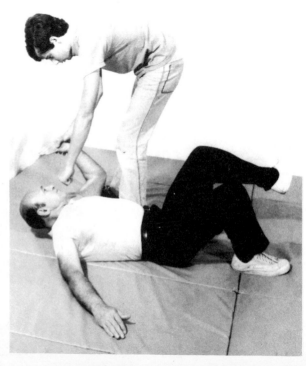

**204**

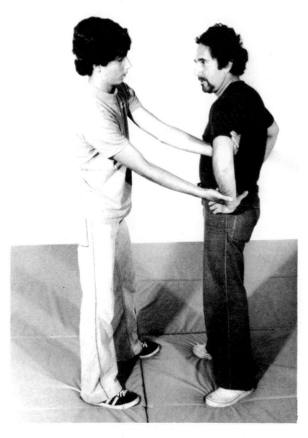

**205**

**206**

**Figs. 205-208** Hammerlock and stranglehold. The opponent is facing the child with hands on hips. The child assumes the hands-up position. The child whips both hands out and grasps the opponent's left wrist with his right hand. The left hand grasps underneath the back of the opponent's arm (Fig. 206). The child, still holding wrist with right hand, pulls back with left hand as though

207

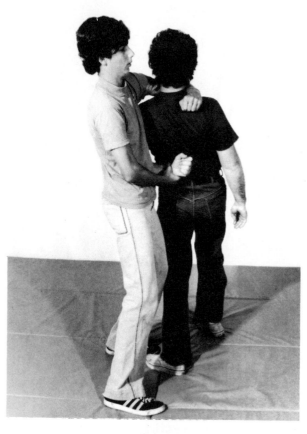

208

pulling back a bow. This will turn the opponent around so that his back will be facing the child (Fig. 207). He now releases his left hand from his arm and places it around his opponent's neck (Fig. 208). From this position he can bring him down to the ground if necessary.

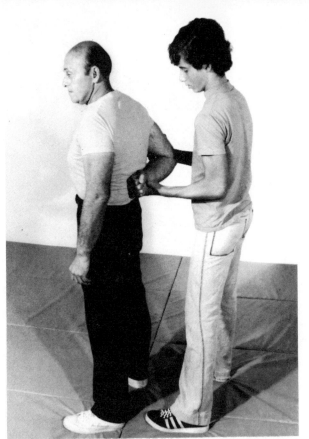

209

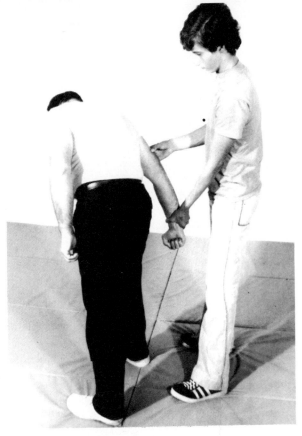

210

**Figs. 209-211**  Hammerlock counter. The child is holding the parent in a right-hand hammerlock. You counter this by bending the body forward and suddenly straightening the right arm downward (Fig. 210). Pull right arm strongly forward and away from opponent's grasp (Fig. 211).

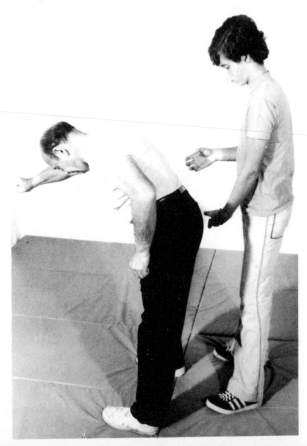

211

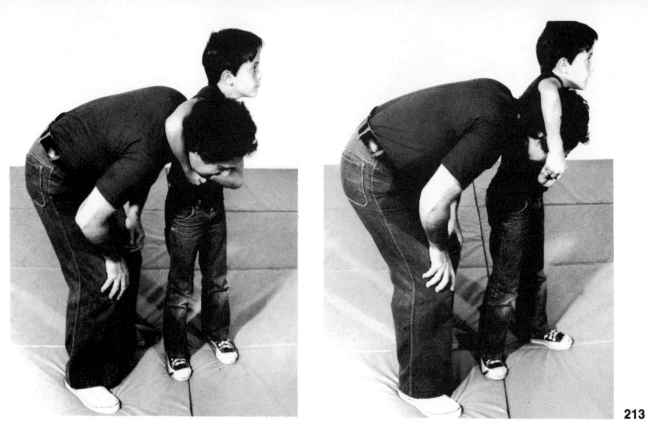

**212**

**213**

**Figs. 212-214**   The wrong way to apply a headlock. The child is grasping the parent around the chin. He cannot apply pressure this way (Fig. 212). In Fig. 213 the child is applying the headlock in the correct manner. The arms are now around the head and ears. Pressure can now be applied by squeezing in toward the chest.

**214**

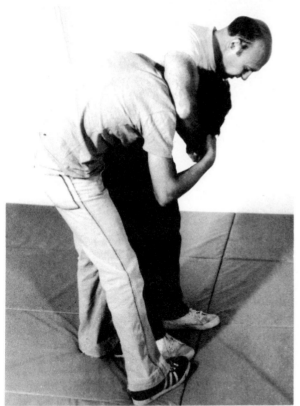

215

216

**Figs. 215-217**   Counter to a side headlock. Your opponent has you in a side headlock. Your left hand goes around your opponent's waist and you grasp his right wrist with your right hand. Take a short step in with your right foot toward your opponent's right foot (Fig. 215). Now take a long step with your left foot and block your opponent's left ankle (Fig. 216). Now throw your opponent over your left ankle and punch to the nose if necessary (Fig. 217).

217

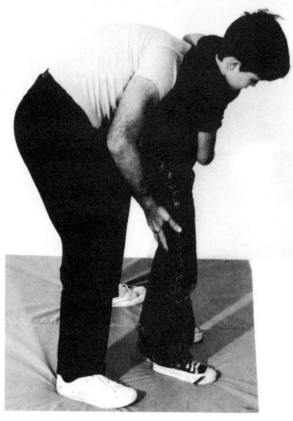

218

**Figs. 218-221** Rear headlock counter. Your opponent has you in a headlock and you are directly behind him. Place the palms of both your hands directly behind the back of your opponent's thighs, right above the knees (Fig. 218). Now sit back and throw your opponent over your head (Fig. 220). Complete the

219

**220**

throw over your head and away from you (Fig. 221). Do not start the throw until you are sitting down. When your opponent is near your face, throw him quickly over your head.

**221**

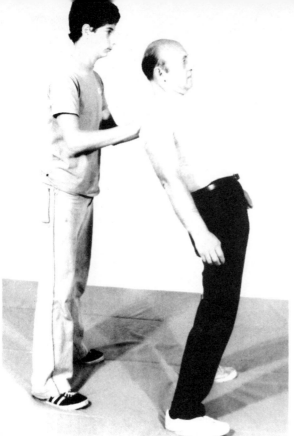

**222**

**223**

**Figs. 222-225**  The four photos on this page show different off-balance positions used to throw your opponent to the ground. Fig. 222: Pulling opponent backward from the shoulders. Fig. 223: Breaking opponent's balance on the right side. Fig. 224: Pulling opponent off balance on the left side. Fig. 225: Pulling opponent forward off balance. In order to throw your opponent to the ground it is essential to first pull him off balance, where he is in a weakened position and cannot use his full strength.

**224**

**225**

226

227

**Figs. 226-229** Shoulder and ankle block. The parent and child in a balanced position, grasping each other's upper arms. The child pulls the parent forward off balance on the right side and blocks the back of the ankle with the back of his right foot (Fig. 227) and throws the parent down over his right foot (Fig. 228). Still holding the parent's right arm the child can punch to the nose if necessary.

228

229

**230**

**231**

**Figs. 230-233**  Underchin and ankle block. Starting from a balanced position, pull your opponent off balance on the right side and block the back of his right ankle with the back of your right foot. Place your right hand underneath your opponent's chin (Fig. 231). Fig. 232 shows the opponent being thrown and Fig. 233 shows the finish of the throw and possible hit to face.

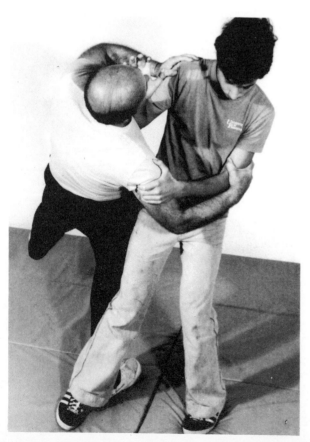

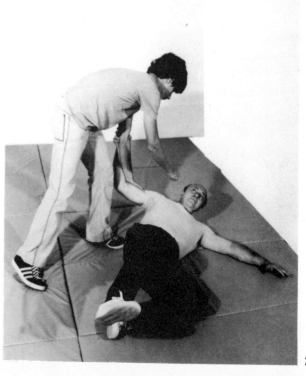

**232**

**233**

234

235

**Figs. 234-236**  Hand waist throw and ankle block. From a balanced position, pull your opponent off balance on the right side. Place your right hand on opponent's right side of waist and block the back of his right ankle with the back of your right foot (Fig. 235). Throw opponent to ground, with possible follow through with punch to face (Fig. 236).

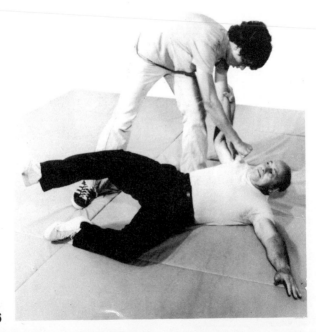

236

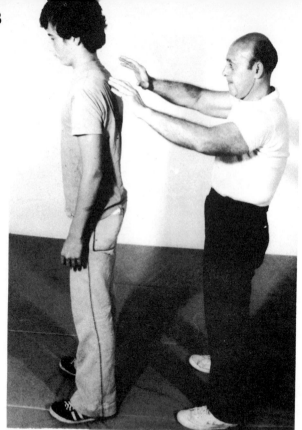

**237**

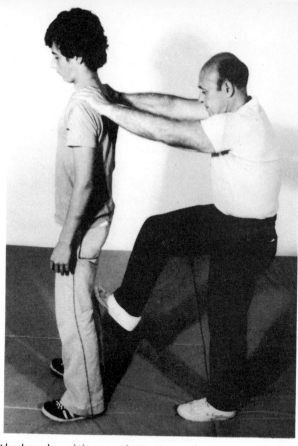

**238**

**Figs. 237-240**   Pull down from behind. Fig. 237 shows the hand position ready to grasp the shoulders. Fig. 238: Both hands grasp shoulders and at the same time the right toe is placed on the back of the knee. Fig. 239: Push the knee in with your toe and at the same time pull the shoulders back. Pull hard enough to bring the opponent down to the ground.

**239**

**240**

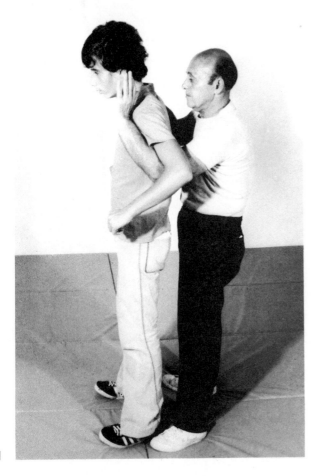 

**Figs. 241-242**   Full nelson counter. Your opponent is bringing his arms underneath your arms, trying to apply a full nelson. Immediately tighten your arms against your sides, pinning his arms against your body (Fig. 242). For counter attack see Figs. 161-162.

120

**243 244**

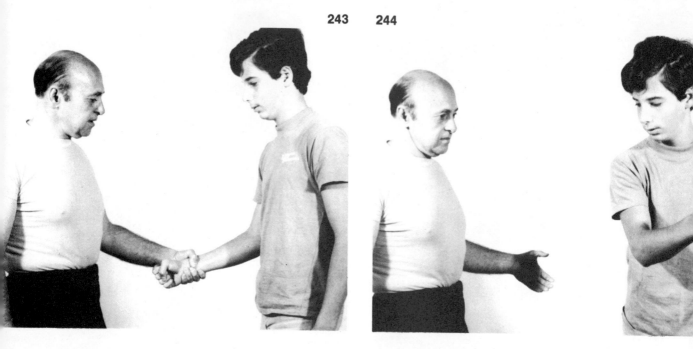

**Figs. 243-246** Counters for wrist grab. Parent holding right wrist with the left hand. To escape this hold you must pull away from the parent's fingertips. Fig. 244 shows the child pulling away from the parent's grasp with speed and force. Figs. 245-246 show another wrist grab counter. Bring your thumb away from your index finger, then quickly snap your hand upward and grab your opponent's wrist.

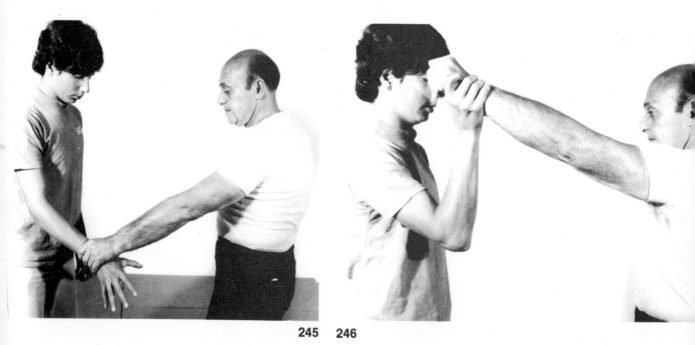

**245 246**

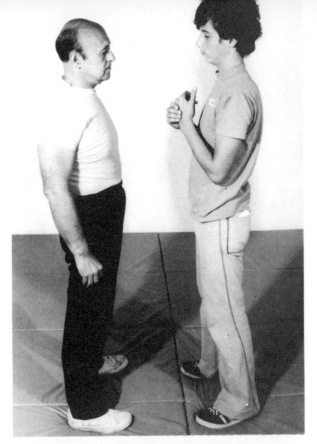

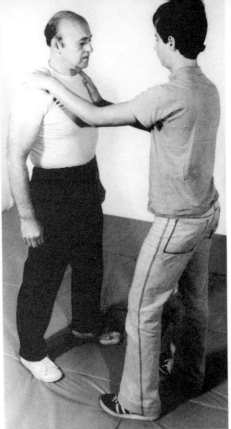

247

248

**Figs. 247-251** Hands shoulder push, stranglehold and bring down. You are facing your opponent in the hands up position. Quickly place your left hand behind opponent's right shoulder and your right hand in front of left shoulder (Fig. 248). Quickly push opponent's left shoulder back as you pull around on right shoulder, turning opponent around (Fig. 249). Opponent's back is now

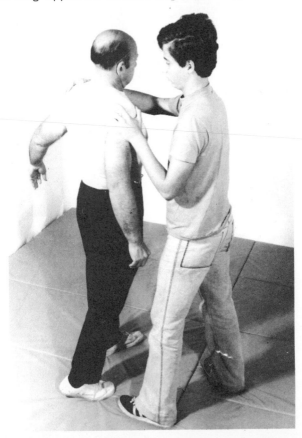

249

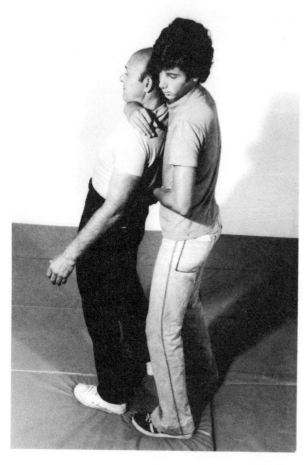

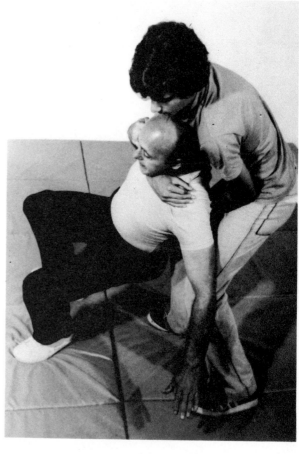

turned to you and the right hand which was in front of the left shoulder is placed around his neck in a stranglehold (Fig. 250). Now place your left hand on the small of his back (Fig. 251). From this position push your opponent's back forward and bring him down to the ground.

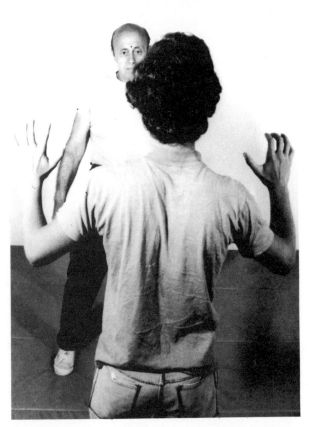

252

253

**Figs. 252-255** Counter to rush attack. Your opponent is rushing at you with hands outstretched. Just before he tries to grasp you, grab him underneath the upper part of his arms (Fig. 254) and step back with your left foot, making a quarter turn to the left, feet parallel. As you do this throw him quickly away from you with force (Fig. 255).

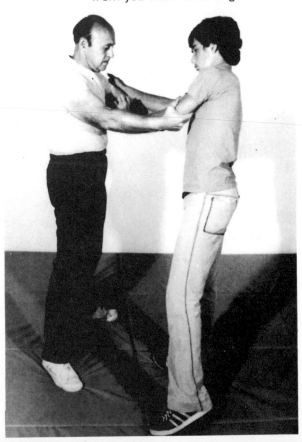

254

255

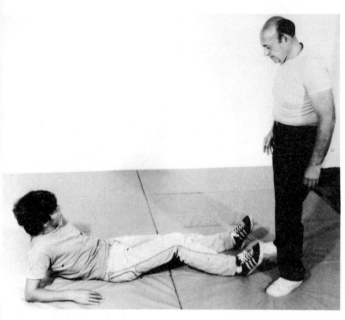

**256**

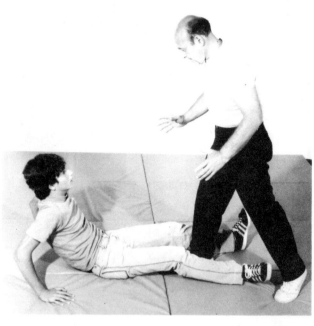

**257**

**Figs. 256-259**   Counter to lying down attack (I). You are lying down on the ground. Your opponent steps in between your legs (Fig. 257). Block his right ankle with your left foot (Fig. 258) and swing your right foot into the side of his right knee (Fig. 259). This will bring him down to the ground.

**258**

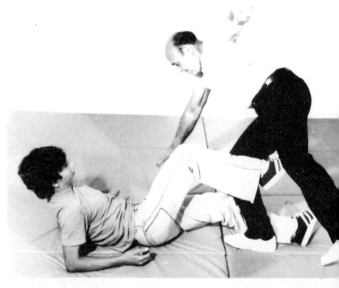

**259**

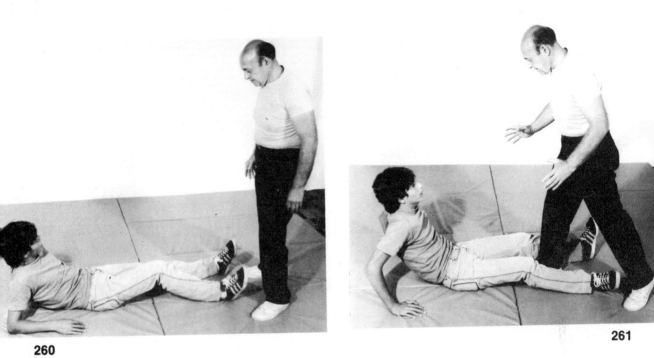

260

261

**Figs. 260-263**   Counter to lying down attack (II). You are lying down on the ground and your opponent steps in between your legs. You block his right ankle with your left ankle and place your right foot against the inside of his right knee (Fig. 262) and push your foot forward and toward the side (Fig. 263), bringing your opponent to the ground.

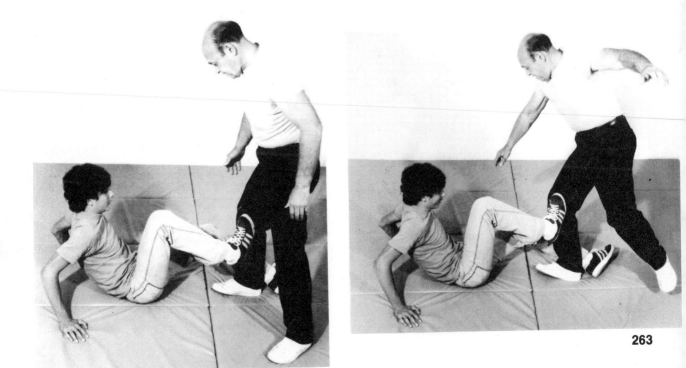

262

263

264

**Figs. 264-267** Counter for sitting on stomach. Your opponent has you down on the floor; he is sitting on your stomach and holding your wrists. You suddenly straighten both your arms out to the side (Fig. 265). This movement will

265

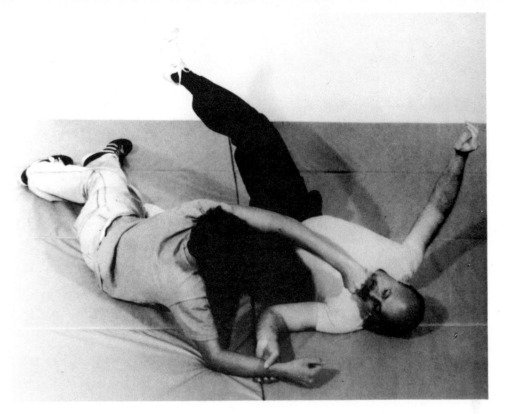

**266**

cause him to fall forward. As he falls forward, turn and push him over to either the left side or right side (Fig. 266). Then punch to face.

**267**

# STRENGTH EXERCISES
# FOR SELF-DEFENSE

Strength and physical fitness is a must for those interested in self-defense. When you are physically strong you have a better chance to succeed in defending yourself. Most children who are continually bullied are usually weak and lack self-confidence. The exercises as outlined in this book will help them gradually build up their strength. This increase in strength will in turn help them gain self-confidence in their ability to defend themselves.

Exercise requires a certain amount of self-discipline. You will find that children from ages five to thirteen will require overseeing. A parent can make exercising more interesting by working out with his child. Most fathers do very little in the way of exercise. The last time they probably did any form of physical activity, such as playing sports, was in high school or college. Here is an opportunity for the parent to get back in shape and become really physically fit.

Though the emphasis in this book is self-defense, I feel very strongly that being physically fit all of your life is very important. You as a parent could influence your child on the necessity of being in a healthy physical condition. It will not only help in self-defense, but it will also aid in all sports. We all inherit our physical structure and strengths or lack of them from our parents or grandparents. Fortunately, with exercise, we can do something to improve ourselves.

No matter how weak you are at present, exercise and diet as outlined in this book will help build up your strength and physique. The educational system does not cater to the weak and underdeveloped child. The physical education of most schools consists of sports such as baseball, football, basketball, soccer, and wrestling. They cater to those who are big and strong and well co-ordinated, and the physical education teachers are in constant search for those boys who can play for the school teams. They do have a physical training program which consists of calisthenics. These exercises include situps, legups, pushups, chinups, etc. Many schools have purchased a Universal Gym which includes various weight-training exercises. When these are done properly in combination with a good diet, they can be of great help in building up your child. However, the school system is overcrowded and it is impossible to obtain the proper attention for each child. The weak and underdeveloped students are made to compete with the strong and athletic students. They soon develop an inferiority complex toward exercise and sports and become an easy prey to bullies.

You *can* be stronger and improve your physique, but it requires a desire on your part to develop and strengthen your body. Then you must discipline yourself to a schedule of diet and exercise. There are three ingredients to a strong well-developed body. They are, in order, proper exercise, diet, and sleep. When you exercise you break down tissues, which you rebuild with nourishing food and sleep. All this helps you to build muscle. It is most important that a youngster should get at least eight to nine hours of sleep. I am astonished when I hear that some parents permit their children to stay up until midnight when they have to get up to go to school at seven A.M. the next morning. You must impress upon your child that if he or she wants to be strong and healthy it is important to get the proper amount of sleep.

I have found that most of my students have difficulty in doing pushups and chinups. These are strength exercises: Pushups require strong triceps (back of upper arm) and pectoral muscles (Figs. 272-273). Chinups utilize the latissimus dorsi (Figs. 278-279) (upper back) and biceps (front of upper arm). Pushups are especially important in conditioning for boxing, judo, karate, and all sports. They will enable your child to hit with more power in boxing and karate. At the same time they will develop his arms and chest. You should see improvement in this area after one month of regular exercise. Children who can do regular pushups should do about five to ten repetitions each day. After the first week they should try to do as many repetitions as they can without straining. It is important for improved strength that you try to increase the number of repetitions each week. You should try to work up to 25 repetitions. Those of you who want to become extremely strong should try to gradually work up to 50 pushups or more. Increased strength can be obtained by doing as many pushups as you possibly can, and repeating the exercise two to ten times each day. Each time an exercise is repeated it is called a set. The average person can obtain good results by doing three sets a day. Those of you who are more ambitious can try doing more than three sets. The more sets you can get into your workout the stronger you will become. However, you must add only one set a week to your workout; it must be done on a gradual basis.

There are a great many children who cannot do a single pushup. They find it very embarrassing when they are asked by their physical education teacher to demonstrate how well they can do the exercise. These children can be helped. The exercise should be approached in three stages. First the children must get their arms stronger by doing a milder form of the pushup. This first stage is done in the following manner: Lie flat on your stomach. Put your hands next to your shoulders in pushup position (Fig. 268). Bring your lower legs up to a 90-degree angle, keeping knees on floor. Push your body up slowly to arms length (Fig. 269). Now lower your body slowly to the floor. The slower the exercise is done the stronger you will become. This type of pushup is easier to accomplish because there is less of the body to push up. This will only be a temporary method. When the child can do this twenty times, the next step will be doing the pushup lying flat on the floor (Fig. 270).

Lie flat on your stomach. Put your hands next to your shoulders in the pushup position. Now slowly push up to arm's length (Fig. 271). Bring your body down and touch the floor. The pushup done in this manner is more difficult. If your child has any trouble pushing up to arm's length, have the child hold his head up high. This will make the pushup easier. After working up to twenty repetitions, your child will be ready to do regular pushups. These are done with body completely straight and off the floor (Fig. 272). Now lower your body slowly with the chest nearly touching the floor (Fig. 273). Then push up slowly to arm's length. For proper amount of repetitions see Figs. 272-273.

The parent must watch for proper form when the child is doing pushups. Since children's arms are weak, they will have a tendency to throw or jerk their bodies upward. You must impress upon them to push their bodies up slowly. Their arms will only get stronger when they do the exercise in this manner.

Chinning is a very difficult exercise for many children and impossible for others. Chinups are an excellent exercise. They are helpful in gaining weight and building up the upper back muscles and biceps. If the parent finds that his child has difficulty or cannot perform this exercise, he can help by teaching the child to do the chinups in three stages. But before you start you must buy a doorway chinning bar with clamps to prevent the bar from slipping. This item can be purchased in most sporting goods stores and the bar can be attached to any doorway. To obtain the correct height, have the child sit on the floor and extend both arms overhead to arm's length. Place the bar at this height. First put on the clamps and then tighten the bar so that it is set firmly, but not so tight that it cannot be removed easily.

Now the child is ready for the first stage. He must lift himself up so that his chin goes up to the bar, being sure that his heels are always in contact with the floor (Figs. 274-275). The exercise should be done five to ten times, depending upon the strength of the child. After the first week this should be repeated twice a day, and the following week three times daily. The repetitions should be increased gradually. The child will become stronger by doing three to five sets a day. When he can chin 15 to 20 repetitions in this manner, he can proceed to the next stage.

The next progressive step is to chin from a standup position (Fig. 276). The bar is put about four inches from the top of the doorway, and the exercise is done in the following manner: The child pulls his body upward until his chin is up to the bar (Fig. 277). Then he lowers his body slowly until his feet touch the floor, or stool if necessary. The parent must watch that the child does not bend his knees or take a little jump to help in doing the chin. The pullup must be done with the arms and back muscles and not the legs. This exercise should be done five to ten times and then gradually increased to 20 repetitions. The sets should be increased from two to five.

The child should now be strong enough to proceed to the final stage and chin with the feet off the floor (Figs. 278-279). In this final stage all the repetitions are performed without the feet ever touching the floor. If you find that the pullup is not being done in perfect form, don't worry about it. Some children do not straighten out their arms, as they find it easier to do the chin with bent arms. Let them do it this way for the time being. Eventually as they become stronger they will perform this exercise in correct form. This type of chin should be done five to ten times per set. Begin with two sets a day and work up to five sets. Your child will be in good shape when he can do 25 correct pushups and ten to 15 chins.

The jump squat is an excellent exercise for developing and strengthening the front thighs and calves. It also helps the individual to run faster and increases the chest size. It should be done in the following manner: Bend down into a half squat (half knee bend) (Fig. 281). Now jump up as high as you can (Fig. 282) and come down immediately into a half squat. Do not land on flat feet, but try to come down on the balls of your feet first and then the heels. This is a continuous exercise, there is no stopping. When it is done in this way it leaves you gasping for breath, and this heavy breathing helps increase the size of the rib cage. Begin this exercise with ten repetitions and gradually work up to 20 or 25. After the first week add another set, and add another set the following week. This will make three sets a day.

If you should have difficulty doing the jump squats, just do the half squats (half knee bends) without jumping (Figs. 299-300). Do the same number of repetitions. When your legs become stronger, try doing the jump squats.

The pushups, chins, and the jump squats are strength builders. The parent must see that the child specializes in these three exercises by doing them in sets. The following exercises can be done in one set:

1. *Abdominal Exercise*—The situps (Figs. 287-288) and legups (Figs 291-292) are important exercises for strengthening the abdomen. The situps strengthen the upper abdomen and the legups the lower abdomen. Strong stomach muscles are necessary for good digestion and good posture and help make punches to this region less painful. If you have not done situps and legups before, begin with five to ten repetitions and gradually work up to 25. Start the situps by lying flat on your back with hands overhead, then sit up by swinging your arms forward toward your toes (Figs. 285-286). It is not necessary to touch your toes. After you can do this 25 times, try to do the exercise with hands behind head (Figs. 287-288). Go back to ten

repetitions and gradually increase it to 25.

There are some children who cannot do even one situp. They can be helped by holding their hands and their ankles (Fig. 283) and then assisting them in sitting up by gently and slowly pulling forward until the situp is accomplished (Fig. 284). After a few weeks of doing ten to 15 repetitions, the child should be ready to do overhead situps. When you find that your child has trouble in a particular exercise, it should be practiced in two to three sets. Always start with a few repetitions and gradually increase the amount as the child becomes stronger.

The legups are done in this manner: Lie flat on your back, holding your hands along the sides of your body (Fig. 291). Lift both legs straight up to a 90-degree angle (Fig. 292) and slowly return them to the floor. Children that find this difficult can bring their knees back to their chest (Figs. 289-290). It is an easier exercise and it strengthens the same muscles as the legups. After about a month, the child can switch to doing legups.

Incidentally the legups should not be done by anyone who has a bad back. This exercise seems to aggravate the lower back muscles. However, the knees back to chest is a good lower abdominal exercise and does not affect the lower back.

2. *Back Exercise*—The back exercise develops and strengthens the spinal muscles of the back. When done regularly it will help prevent back trouble. This exercise is done with the child lying on his stomach on the floor with hands clasped behind the back. The parent should hold the child's ankles (Fig. 295). The child should then lift his head and shoulders upward as high as possible (Fig. 296). Repeat this ten times and gradually increase it to 25. To make this exercise progressively harder, place the hands behind the neck (Figs. 297-298). Do ten repetitions and gradually increase it to 25.

3. *Posture Exercises*—Parents are constantly worried about their child's posture. He may slouch or walk with one shoulder lower than the other. This type of posture sometimes comes from carrying books on one side. The child develops one side of his body while the other side remains weak. Books must be carried equally on the left and right side. This will strengthen both side muscles and help correct the situation.

An excellent exercise for good posture is the shoulder shrug. This exercise can be done with or without weights. If done with weights (Figs. 305-306), it develops and strengthens to a greater degree the trapezius muscles that help hold the shoulders back.

Do the exercise by bringing the shoulders up towards the ears and then rolling the shoulders backwards. Some people have difficulty in rolling the shoulders backward. If your child has this problem, having him bring his shoulders up to the ears and down will accomplish the same result.

The exercises necessary for good posture are shoulder shrugs, situps, legups, the side exercise, and the back exercise. Unless the back and the abdominal muscles are strong it is very difficult to maintain good posture. Although these exercises are important for good posture, it is also necessary for children to be reminded to stand up straight. The stomach should be held in and shoulders back. They may rebel at first at the reminder, but when they grow up they will appreciate what you have done for them.

While doing all exercises, breathe freely through the mouth. Do not hold your breath in any of the exercises.

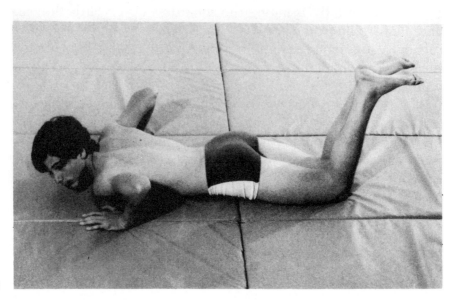

**268**

**Figs. 268-269**  Beginner's pushups. All pushups help to develop and strengthen the back of the arms (triceps) and chest muscles (pectorals). Fig. 268 shows the first step toward getting your arms stronger for pushups. Lie face down on the floor, hands shoulder-width apart, legs bent back at a 90-degree angle. Slowly push up to arm's length. Lower your body slowly to the floor. The exercise must be done slowly to be effective. Do not jerk or throw your body up. Begin with five to ten repetitions. Add two repetitions a week until you can do 20 repetitions. Repeat this exercise three times a day. Each time you repeat the exercise, it is called a set.

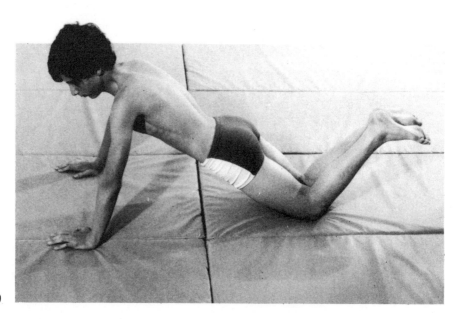

**269**

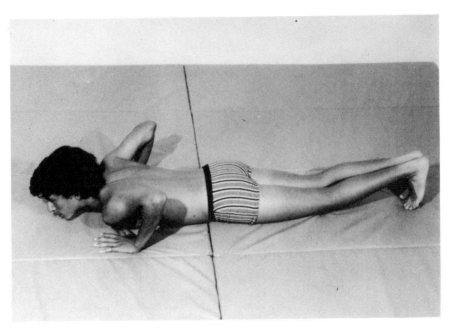

**270**

**Figs. 270-271** Intermediate pushups. Lie face down on the floor with hands shoulder-width apart, feet straight out a few inches apart. Slowly push your body straight up to arm's length. Return to the floor slowly. If you have trouble pushing your body to arm's length from this position, try keeping your head higher off the floor. Begin with five to ten repetitions. Add two repetitions a week until you can do 20 repetitions. Do three sets a day.

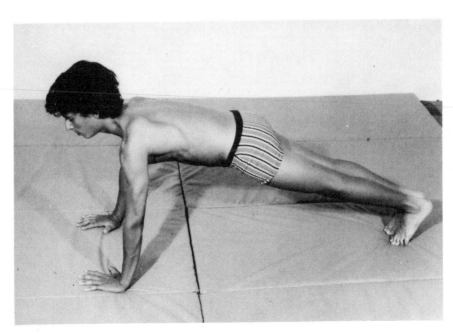

**271**

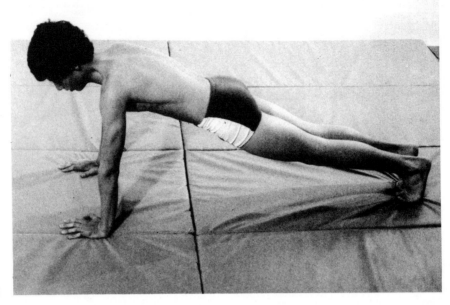

**272**

**Figs. 272-273**   Regular pushups. Start this exercise off the floor at arm's length, body straight out, feet a few inches apart. Slowly lower your body until it is close to the floor. Push up slowly until you are at arm's length. Begin with five to ten repetitions. Add two repetitions a week until you can do 20 to 25. Do three sets a day. If you are interested in becoming exceptionally strong, try to work up to ten sets. This will probably bring up your pushups to 50 or more.

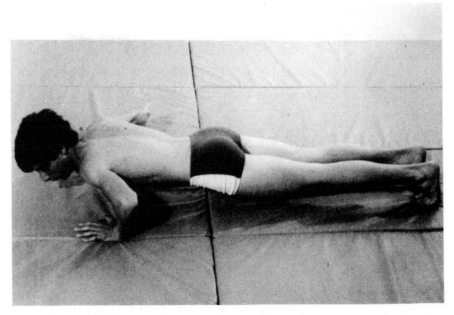

**273**

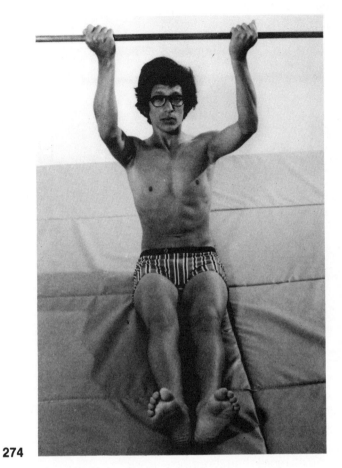

274

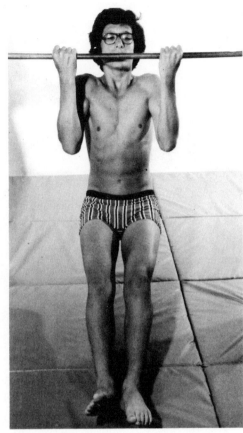

275

**Figs. 274-275**  Chinups (beginners). Chinups strengthen and develop the upper back muscles (latissimus dorsi). Chinups are a very difficult exercise. Children who have trouble doing regular chins will be able to do so through gradual stages: Sit on the floor, feet extended. Using underhand grip, grasp the bar at near arm's length. If possible have someone hold your ankles. Now pull up slowly until chin is over the bar, then lower yourself slowly. Begin with two to ten repetitions. Add two repetitions a week until you can do 20. Do three sets a day. After a month, if you are a little more ambitious work up to five sets a day.

140

**276**

**Figs. 276-277** Chinups (intermediate). Stand on floor. Using an underhand grip, grasp chinning bar at almost arm's length. Pull yourself up slowly until your chin is over the bar. Lower your body slowly until your feet touch the floor. Begin with five to ten repetitions. Add two repetitions a week until you can do 20. Do three sets a day. If after a while you can do more than three sets a day, do so.

**277**

**278**

**Figs. 278-279**   Chinups (regular). Jump up and grasp the chinning bar with an underhand grip. Pull yourself up slowly until your chin is over the bar. Lower yourself slowly until you are back at arm's length and continue chinning. Do not touch floor. Begin with five to ten repetitions. Add two repetitions a week until you can do 15. Do three sets a day. If you are interested in becoming stronger in this exercise, increase to five sets a day.

**279**

142

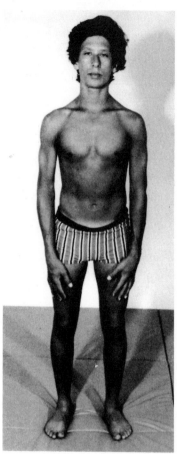
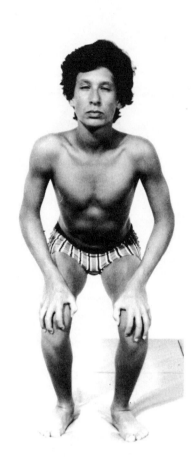
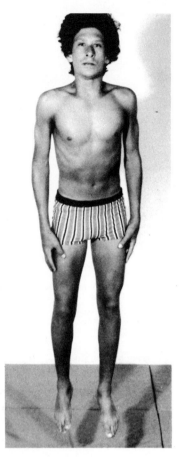

**280**
**281**
**282**

**Figs. 280-282** Jump squats. Jump squats are done to develop and strengthen the thigh, calf and chest muscles. Stand erect with feet about 12 inches apart. Squat down into a half knee bend, hands on fronts of thighs. Now leap straight up as high as you can. Come down immediately into a knee bend. This is a continuous jump; there is no stopping between jumps. Begin with ten repetitions. Add two repetitions a week until you reach 20. Do two to three sets a day.

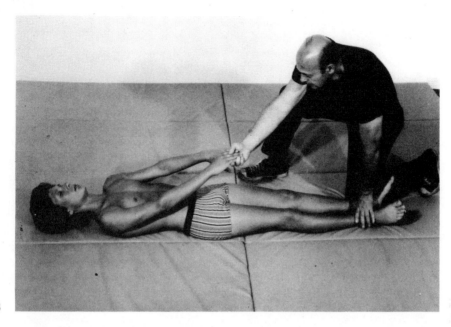

283

**Figs. 283-284**  Situps (for weak stomach muscles). Situps help to develop and strengthen the upper abdominals. The child lies on his back on the floor and the parent holds both hands and both ankles of the child. The child tries to sit up. If he cannot, the parent helps him by pulling him up slowly. Return to original position. Begin with five to ten repetitions. Add two repetitions a week until you reach 20. Do two to four sets a day. After two to four weeks the child should be able to sit up without help.

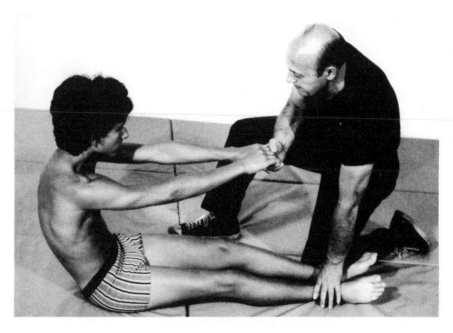

284

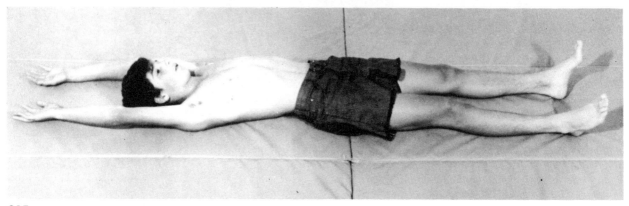

**285**

**Figs. 285-286** Situps (regular). Lie on your back on the floor, feet stretched out, arms overhead. Swing your arms forward, lifting your back off the floor, and bringing your hands toward your toes. Return to original position and repeat. Begin with five to ten repetitions. Add two repetitions a week until you reach 20.

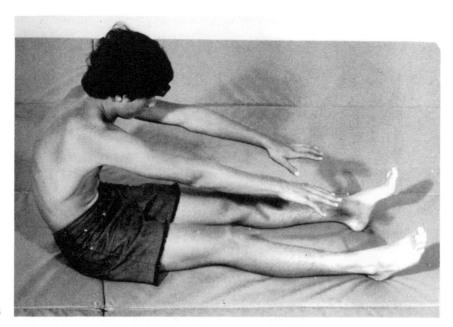

**286**

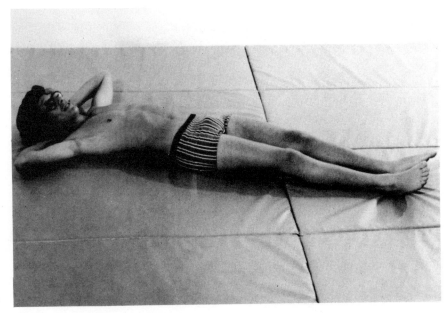

**287**

**Figs. 287-288**    Situps (Advanced). Lie on your back on the floor, feet stretched out, hands behind your neck. Sit up to a 90-degree angle. Return to original position and repeat. Begin with five to ten repetitions. Add two a week until you reach 20.

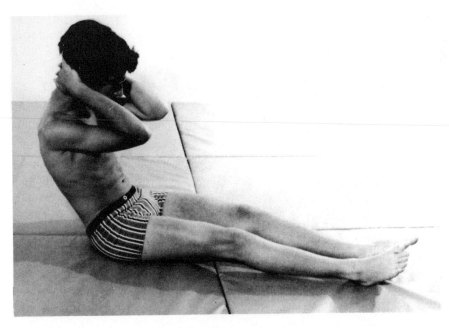

**288**

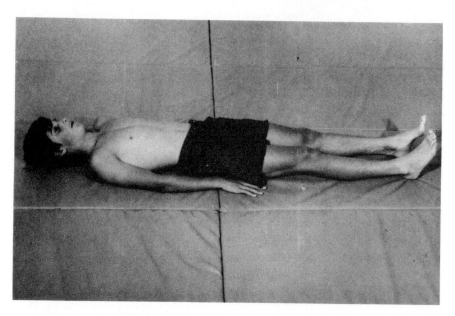

289

**Figs. 289-290**  Knees back to chest. This develops and strengthens lower abdominals. Lie on your back on the floor, feet stretched out, arms alongside body. Bend your knees and bring them back toward your chest. Return to original position and repeat. Begin with ten repetitions. Add two repetitions a week until you reach 20.

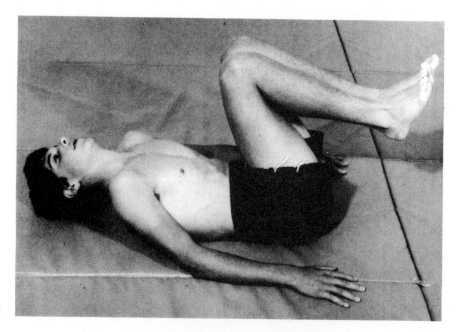

290

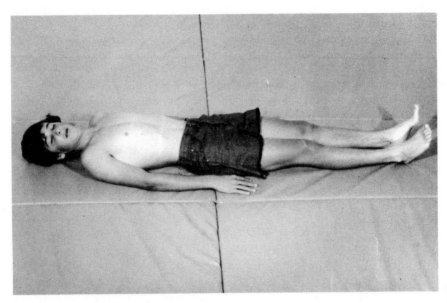

**291**

**Figs. 291-292**  Legups. Legups strengthen and develop lower abdominals. Lie on your back on the floor, feet stretched out, hands alongside your body. Bring both legs straight up to a 90-degree angle. Return to original position. Begin exercise with five to ten repetitions. Add two repetitions a week until you reach 20.

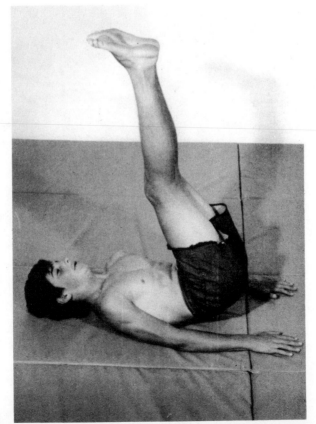

**292**

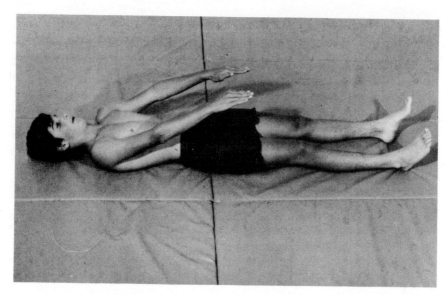

**293**

**Figs. 293-294**  Combination situp and legup. This develops and strengthens upper and lower abdominal muscles. Lie on your back on the floor, feet stretched out, hands held straight out over your body. Bring your body and your legs up together about 12 inches off the floor. Return to the original position and repeat. Begin with five to ten repetitions. Add two repetitions a week until you reach 20.

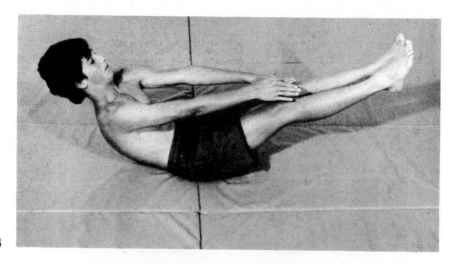

**294**

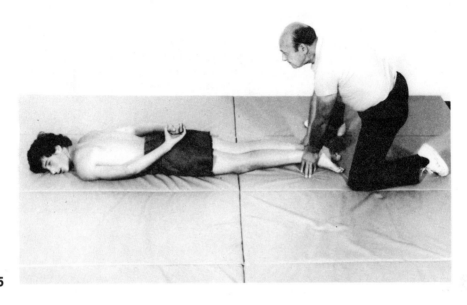

**295**

**Figs. 295-296** Back exercise (beginners). This develops the back muscles (erector spinal). Lie on the floor on your stomach, feet outstretched, hands clasped behind the back. Have someone hold your ankles. Bring your head and shoulders up as high as possible. Return to original position and repeat. Begin with ten repetitions. Add two repetitions a week until you reach 20.

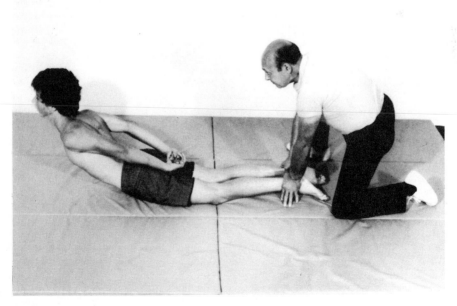

**296**

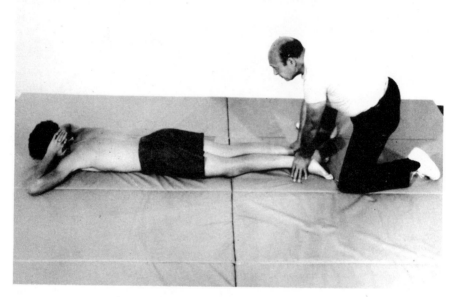

297

**Figs. 297-298**  Back exercise (advanced). Lie on the floor on your stomach, feet outstretched. Have someone hold your ankles. Clasp your hands behind your neck. Bring your head and shoulders up as high as possible. Return to original position and repeat. Begin with ten repetitions. Add two repetitions a week until you reach 20.

298

**299**

**Figs. 299-300**   Knee bend. Knee bends develop and strengthen thigh and hip muscles. Stand with feet 12 inches apart, arms outstretched for balance. Bend your legs and lower your body to a half squat. Return to original position and repeat. Begin with ten repetitions. Add two repetitions a week until you reach 20.

**300**

152

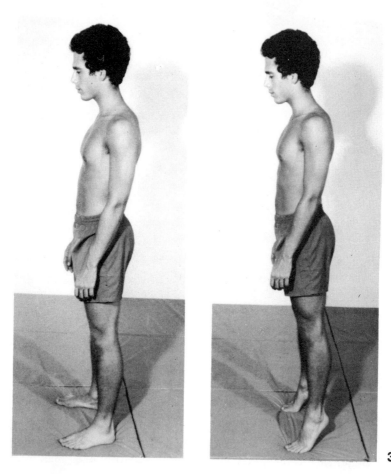

301

302

**Figs. 301-302**  Rise on toes. This develops and strengthens the calf muscles and arches and ankles. Stand with feet 12 inches apart. Rise on your toes as high as possible. Return to original position. Begin with ten repetitions. Add two repetitions a week until you reach 20.

**303**        **304**

**Figs. 303-304**    Side exercise. This develops and strengthens the side muscles (external obliques). Hold a ten-pound dumbbell in right hand. Bend to right side. Bring body over to left side. Keep moving from side to side without stopping. Repeat exercise with left hand. If you do not have a dumbbell use a heavy book. Begin with ten repetitions. Add two repetitions a week until you reach 20.

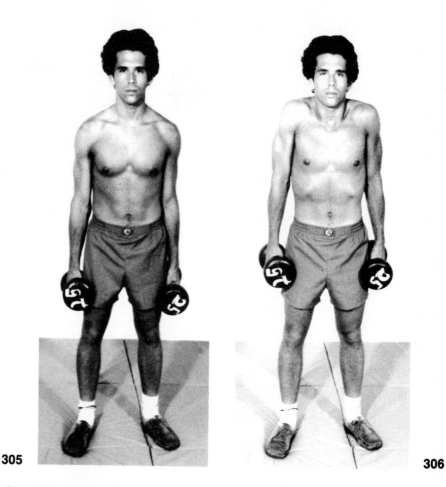

305

306

**Figs. 305-306**   Shoulder shrug. This develops and strengthens upper back muscles (trapezius). Stand with two ten-pound dumbbells in each hand, feet 12 inches apart. Raise your shoulders upward in a shrug-like movement; try to touch your ears with your shoulders. Then try to roll your shoulders backward. Return to original position and repeat. If you do not have dumbbells, use two heavy books. Begin with ten repetitions. Add two repetitions a week until you reach 20.

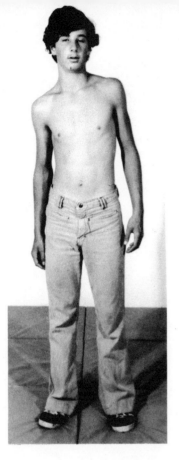

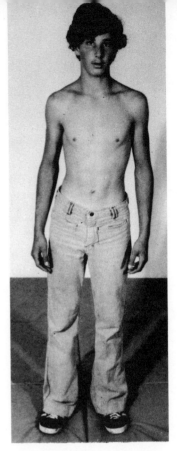

307

308

**Figs. 307-310**  Correct and incorrect posture. Fig. 307 shows child with right shoulder lower than left shoulder. Fig. 308 shows correct posture. Fig. 309 shows child with shoulders too far forward. Fig. 310 shows correct posture. All of the previous exercises help to correct poor posture.

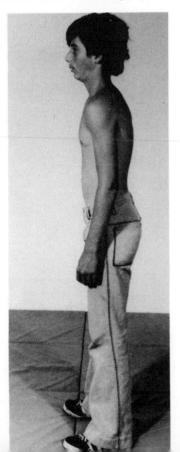

309

310

# REDUCING AND
# WEIGHT GAINING
# FOR SELF-DEFENSE

It is difficult for underweight children to put on weight because they seem to lack the appetite for food. Therefore, they must be encouraged to eat more. The diet in this book plus the exercises that will help increase the size of their muscles will lead to the desired weight gain.

The way to gain weight is to develop the largest muscles of the body, such as the thighs, hips, latissimus dorsi (upper back muscles), and pectorals (chest muscles). The exercises that are involved are chinning for the back muscles (Figs. 278-279), squat jumps for the thighs and hips (Figs. 280-282), pushups for the pectorals and triceps (Figs 272-273). These are the weight-gaining exercises and from three to five sets or more must be done every other day. Children who are on the weight-gaining diet should exercise a day and rest the next day, and they should not participate in sports that involve a tremendous amount of running. This would only help in keeping their weight down.

Parents must not try to give enormous meals to their children. Instead they should, if possible, have them eat as much as they can five or six times a day. It is easier for their stomachs to digest their food in this way.

*Breakfast* should consist of orange juice, two eggs, two pieces of toast, and a glass of milk. Some children do not like eggs but

157

will accept them in French toast. If you are planning to give the child dry cereal, add a banana, nuts, and dates. This will make the breakfast more nutritious and will add extra calories. Don't forget to include the orange juice and two pieces of toast with cereal.

*Lunch* should consist of a tuna fish sandwich with a cheese sandwich or any two sandwiches with protein food such as meat or fish, plus a glass of milk. When the child comes home from school, the parent should prepare a sandwich such as peanut butter with or without jam with a glass of milk.

*Dinner* should consist of meat, fowl, or fish, salad, vegetables, carbohydrates such as spaghetti, potatoes, corn, etc., milk, and some fresh fruit. There should be an after-dinner snack of a sandwich and glass of milk. The child should try to stay away from junk food such as cookies, candy, soda, cake, etc.

Milk is an excellent food for gaining weight. A child who is underweight should start with a quart of milk a day and gradually increase this to two quarts a day. There is an excellent drink that has helped many of my pupils to increase their weight. The recipe is as follows:

> 2 glasses of milk
> ½ cup of powdered milk
> 2 scoops of ice cream
> 2 tbs. of malt
> 1 banana
> 1 egg

Mix it all in a blender. If the child complains about the taste, try leaving out the banana, or the egg.

Just as overweight people have difficulty in dieting, your child is going to find it hard to eat additional food. The parent must motivate the child by impressing upon him that by gaining weight he will become stronger and be able to defend himself much better. Boxers fight in their own weight class, because the more muscular weight they carry the stronger the punch. You must try to drive home the fact that exercising and eating properly will help develop strength and an outstanding physique.

Overweight children also have a difficult problem. There must be a change in their eating habits. They have to eat more protein foods such as meat, fish, eggs, cheese, powdered or skim milk, etc. These foods, when combined with exercise, will build muscles and not fat. They must also eat more vegetables such as stringbeans, carrots, asparagus, etc., plus green salads. Most children have a craving for sweets, but there are many diet drinks and diet dessert foods on the market that can be substituted for them. Once the weight has been brought down to a normal level, more carbohydrates such as bread, corn, potatoes, and some sweets can be eaten.

The parent should weigh the child every second day, so that any unusual weight gain can be noticed. Usually when the youngster is overweight, a parent is also overweight. If this should be the case, the parent can help the child immensely by dieting too. The type of foods that are kept in the house is also extremely important. Fattening foods such as candy, cookies, ice cream, and cake should not be made easily available, although it may be necessary to offer the child some reward, in the form of a treat, as he strives to reach his goal.

The important exercises for the overweight child are the situps (Figs. 285-286), knees back to chest for the abdominal region (Figs. 289-290), the back exercise for the spinal muscles (Figs. 295-296), the side exercise for the external obliques (side muscles) (Figs. 107-108), and the jump squats (knee bends) for the thighs and hips (Figs. 280-281). The exercises should start with five repetitions and gradually work up to 25.

Parents should try to interest their child in playing active sports such as tennis, basketball, soccer, and jogging. If the child is very active it will help in weight loss. The youngster should exercise daily as well as go on a low calorie diet that can be prescribed by your doctor. The goal of the parent is to see that the child loses weight and performs the exercises which will strengthen and develop his physique. Children without weight problems and in good physical condition will be more capable of defending themselves.